Project Management
for Planners

A
Practical
Guide

Project Management for Planners

A Practical Guide

By
Terry A. Clark, AICP, PMP

PLANNERS PRESS
AMERICAN PLANNING ASSOCIATION
Chicago, Illinois
Washington, D.C.

Copyright 2002 by the American Planning Association
122 S. Michigan Ave., Suite 1600, Chicago, IL 60603

ISBN (paperback edition): 1-884829-63-5
ISBN (hardbound edition): 1-884829-64-3
Library of Congress Catalog Number 2001-135175
Printed in the United States of America
All rights reserved

Editing and interior composition by Joanne Shwed, Backspace Ink

I dedicate this book to my wife, Susan,
and our two sons, Sam and Max,
who have taught me the true meaning
of love and support.

Contents

Foreword

Project Management for Planners was written to be a practical, hands-on resource to the practicing planner who is also a project manager. It is intended to provide planners with the knowledge of how to bring real-world planning projects to a successful, timely and efficient close. The book gives planners useful guidance not generally offered in more formal educational venues.

The information provided in Part 2 of this book takes the terminology and framework offered in *A Guide to the Project Management Body of Knowledge (PMBOK® Guide), 2000 Edition,* prepared by the Project Management Institute, Inc. (PMI), and puts it in the context of planning. The *PMBOK® Guide* is the professionally accepted standard for project management, although it does not speak directly to planners.

Project Management for Planners does speak directly to planners and uses planning terminology, examples and case studies to give the planner the tools he/she needs to do the job.

AUDIENCE

I wrote *Project Management for Planners* with the public and private sector professional planner in mind—the planner who has just been given a project to manage. The primary audience is the entry- or mid-level planning professional who has been tasked with bringing a top-notch plan in on time and within budget.

The book also speaks to the more experienced planner and the planning manager. Planners in these positions have a tremendous opportunity to develop an environment that uses and supports the project management approach. This can include setting up the organization in a way that assists project managers. It can also include the training and development of planners in the area of project management.

Educators and students are also encouraged to bring *Project Management for Planners* into the college classroom. Planning schools offer their students a tremendous amount of knowledge and insight. The project management realities of meeting time, money and quality standards when preparing plans on the job should be part of planning schools' curricula.

OVERVIEW OF THE CONTENTS

The book is divided into three parts and nine chapters. At the end of each chapter is a review of the chapter's major concepts and ideas. Part 1 includes two chapters. Chapter 1, *Introduction*, is an introduction to the field of project management. It introduces project management concepts and terminology. Chapter 2, *To Managers and Supervisors*, is oriented towards the manager and supervisor. Project management can be applied in an environment that does not recognize its importance or potential. In such an environment, the project manager can still benefit by the application of the process. However, the final product can be of higher quality, completed in less time, and accomplished with fewer resources if the organization's managers and supervisors support the project manager.

Part 2 of the book is divided into five chapters that apply the five process groups of project management as identified in Project Management Institute's *PMBOK® Guide* and put them in the language of planners. The five chapters include Chapter 3, *Initiating*; Chapter 4, *Planning*; Chapter 5, *Executing*; Chapter 6, *Controlling*; and Chapter 7, *Closing*. Each of the five chapters is written to help the professional planner. Fictional interviews are provided at the beginning of each chapter to introduce the concepts that are further described in the text. Resources and job aids are included at the end of each chapter to help the reader build on and apply the information provided in Part 2.

Part 3 of *Project Management for Planners* includes two chapters that offer insights gathered over many years of managing planning projects and project managers. Chapter 8, *Case Studies*, contains four case studies of real-world planning projects, and were chosen to provide the reader with a wide spectrum of project complexity and direction. Chapter 9,

Perspectives, gives the reader some hard-earned advice on how to keep one's sanity when managing planning projects. Managing projects is not easy and it is important for the planner to keep things in perspective.

Preface

Planners are a unique group of professionals dedicated to bettering our world. As planners, we are driven to prepare and implement plans that are living, breathing documents. Our plans must be visionary and daring, while at the same time embraced by local citizens and financially supported by elected officials.

It is not easy to be a good planner. We need all the help we can get. As planning projects become more complex and our "customers" develop increasing expectations, the prospect of producing meaningful and realistic plans becomes more difficult. Planners are constantly riding the slippery slope between idealism and real-world realities.

Project management should be an easy sell to the planning profession. Many planners already use a disciplined approach towards managing projects; however, many of us don't. Project management provides the planner with the necessary tools and processes to bring complex and high-quality planning projects to our customers on time and within budget. Project management provides some structure to the planning process. *Project Management for Planners* offers the professional planner the tools and practical advice on how to be a successful project manager.

Acknowledgements

I can't write another word without mentioning my wife, Susan Clark. She was a constant source of support, love and just the right amount of motivation that I needed to start and complete this book. Writing a book while working full time added a lot of stress to our household and Susan kept our two sons and me pointed in the right direction. She constantly reminded me to enjoy the experience. She's also an excellent editor.

My two sons, Sam and Max, gave me the gift of diversion that I desperately needed at times. Baseball, homework, fishing and neighborhood friends all helped me keep this book project in perspective. My parents, John and Pat Clark, offered support all the way from Tucson, Arizona.

My friends and colleagues at the South Florida Water Management District are too many to mention properly. However, I do want to acknowledge Mark Elsner and Agnes McLean from the South Florida Water Management District, who gave me their precious time to review sections of this book. Debra Case and Patrick Lynch, also from the District, helped me with the graphics and photographs in the book.

Sylvia Lewis and the other staff members of the American Planning Association's Planners Press in Chicago were a delight and a joy to work with.

Last but not least, I want to thank Joanne Shwed for her insightful, accurate and timely editing skills.

—Terry A. Clark
Wellington, Florida
October 2001

An Introduction to Project Management for Planners and Managers

Part 1 of Project Management for Planners *includes two chapters. Chapter 1 presents an introduction and overview of project management. A brief description of the major components of project management is provided along with an explanation of why project management is so important to planners.*

Chapter 2 addresses the line manager and supervisor. If a project manager is to be successful, it is critical that the internal managers, organization and procedures are supportive of the project management methodology. Chapter 2 emphasizes these points and offers managers and supervisors some hints on what they can do to create an environment that is supportive of project managers and teams.

1

Introduction

A good plan today is better than a perfect plan tomorrow.

—FROM THE MOVIE, *WAG THE DOG*

The future belongs to those who believe in the beauty of their dreams.

—ELEANOR ROOSEVELT

One's mind, once stretched by a new idea, never regains its original dimensions.

—OLIVER WENDELL HOLMES

WELCOME

Welcome to the world of project management for planners. Many practicing planners believe that the final planning product justifies the means. If, in a planner's mind, the public could be better served by extending the deadline for a comprehensive plan six more months, then the decision is simple: extend the deadline six more months. At times planners think, "If I could just get the Board of County Commissioners to agree to hire three more planners, then I could do the job right" and "If we could just get the new geographic information system (GIS) online before we started on the land use inventory, we could do a quality plan."

If only, if only, if only . . . if only the world would just stop for a few months, I could get caught up and do the job the way it was meant to be done.

Guess what? The world doesn't work that way. Especially now. Either staffing and budgets are getting cut with workloads increasing, or expectations are expanding much faster than the resources to get the job done. "Do more with less" has become the mantra for most public and private sector organizations.

How are we supposed to accomplish more projects in less time and with fewer resources, review more zoning changes, write more land development codes, *and* involve the public at all levels, *while* maintaining a quality of work that passes scrutiny by our elected officials, clients and taxpayers? The workplace demands placed on planners can be frustrating, debilitating and downright career-threatening. What's a planner to do?

This book outlines a strategy that gives the planner a fighting chance at meeting these expanding—and sometimes unreasonable—expectations. That strategy is *project management*.

NOT NEW

Project management is not new. It has been around for quite some time. Project management was originally developed as a way of organizing and scheduling complex military and construction projects. The processes of building a military force, and constructing bridges and highways, lent themselves well to a structured approach of identifying tasks, timeframes, deliverables and budgets. The tasks were relatively easy to identify and fit into a project management approach. They were fairly easy to sequence, estimate and schedule. The processes were fairly well structured.

Project management has since been adopted as a way of doing business by the information technology (IT) community. Even the creative process of developing new software has benefited greatly by the process-driven application of project management techniques. What was once a maddening maze of software engineers, developers and programmers is now a structured environment of clearly identified goals, schedules and responsibilities. The results show that by applying project management techniques to the IT community, efficiencies and effectiveness have been greatly improved.

IT'S NOT JUST FOR ENGINEERS ANYMORE

The benefits of project management are proven. Project management is an adopted way of doing business by many professions, particularly engineers. So why haven't planners adopted the project management approach for planning projects? That is a good question and one that deserves thoughtful consideration.

Planners usually approach a project with a very clear vision of what they want to accomplish. As planners, we tend to be visionaries. As the saying goes, "If you don't know where you want to go, anyplace will do." A project must have a visionary, and that visionary must communicate that vision to the affected community.

The majority of a planner's time is spent on creating and delivering the vision, with much less energy—in some cases, hardly any energy at all—being spent on achieving the vision. We, as planners, tend to spend too much time in the future and not enough time in the present. That translates into blown project budgets, missed deadlines, impatient elected officials, frustrated members of the public and, sometimes, lost jobs.

Most importantly, when the planner is unable to develop a plan on time and within budget that achieves the vision, the vision gets lost. The plan, if ever completed, is put on the shelf, the public moves on to another crisis, and elected officials find and deal with the culprit.

As planners, we must become competent project managers to achieve our vision. Part of being a planner must include the skills and abilities to efficiently and effectively manage projects. The alternative is lost credibility, job frustration, shrinking budgets and staff, and the increasing inability to achieve the marvelous visions that we have developed. This is simply not acceptable.

Many of the skills that planners possess are directly applicable to project management. In fact, it is estimated that 35% of project management involves planning compared with 25% for execution (see Table 3-1 in Chapter 3). In other words, more time is spent by the project manager on planning the project than making it happen. That is an incredible statistic, especially for planners. The skills required to manage projects are more in line with the planning profession than any other profession, including engineering.

Kerzner (1998, p. 272) estimates that up to 90% of a project manager's time may be spent on communication, with the rest of the time on technical issues. Planners have tremendous skills in communication; we just need to remember to apply our communication skills to the management of our projects, not to just selling the vision.

PROFESSIONAL DEVELOPMENT

Planning is not the only profession that can benefit from learning and applying project management skills and techniques. Demands for increasing efficiencies and effectiveness in all work areas are growing at an extremely rapid pace. Almost all workers are being pressured to perform at higher levels. As a result, new ways of doing business are being adopted by many professions. As mentioned earlier, construction and IT professionals have used project management techniques for quite some time.

Manufacturers, architects, designers and general office workers also see the advantages of using a project management approach. Entire organizations are being reorganized to better support a project management philosophy. Traditional, top-down, hierarchical organizational structures are being turned upside down to reflect a project-driven mission.

The following story highlights the radical approach some organizations take to support a project philosophy. A young project manager at an IT company met the president of the firm on her way into the office one morning. The president said hello and asked how she was doing. Instead of the usual noncommittal greeting, the project manager said that she was having a problem in getting a project deliverable to a client due to unnecessary paperwork in the shipping department. She told the president that she could really use his help in getting that shipment out today because the client was expecting it. The president said he would call the shipping department as soon as he got to his office and asked her if there was anything else he could do to help her.

This story highlights the project-driven organization. The president and the project manager essentially reversed traditional hierarchical roles to ensure that the product got to the client on time. Getting the project deliverable to the client on time was more important than the standard corporate greeting to the president on the way into the office. The president and the project manager both recognized it and both acted to support that belief. As a result, they will have a satisfied client.

You may be thinking that the above example will never work in your office environment. Maybe that's true and maybe it's not. One thing is certain: if planners don't begin to do things differently, we are going to be left on the sidelines by other professionals and organizations that can. Now is the time for us to shine as professionals and adopt a new way of doing business.

THE LATEST FAD?

We have all seen a lot of organizational and professional improvement fads come and go. Total quality management, reengineering and process improvement have come and gone as the latest and greatest ways of improving workplace efficiencies and productivity. While they have obviously had a positive impact at some organizations, they have not enjoyed widespread success or acceptance. These formulaic-driven approaches have suffered from a rigidity that limits their applicability. They look good on paper but, in real-world application, they just don't hold water.

Many people agree that a project management approach can work in a variety of situations and at many levels of an organization. Construction and high-tech firms are currently using project management techniques extensively. At first blush, these two types of organizations don't have a lot in common. One is traditionally a blue-collar environment involving physical labor and "moving dirt" projects. High-tech firms, on the other hand, employ primarily office workers who are highly creative and tend to work independently.

Project management is not just a nice theory developed by a couple of professors and put on the shelf. It is a recognized way of organizing and performing work that has proven applications in a wide variety of work situations. It has been developed by workers to meet an immediate need of increasing efficiencies while producing quality work. It has shown to be flexible and adaptable in many different kinds of organizations. It is time for planners to give project management a fair shake and determine if it fits our profession.

WHAT IS PROJECT MANAGEMENT?

Project management is not a black art practiced by a few knowing witches. Although some people would like us to believe otherwise, it does not involve Harry Potter-like secret potions and equations, nor does it need to be practiced with a robe and pointed hat.

Project Management Institute (PMI) defines project management as "the application of knowledge, skills, tools, and techniques to project activities to meet project requirements." (Project Management Institute, Inc., 2000, p. 6) Project management is a set of tools, or a technology, for producing a deliverable. Simply put, it is a method of organizing information and focusing people towards delivering a product.

Figure 1-1. The Triple Constraint

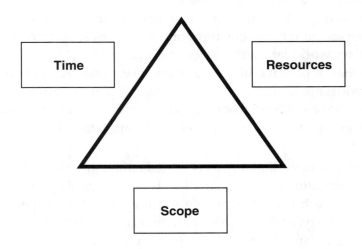

The project management process involves five process groups. Each of the process groups has a distinct purpose and is generally sequential:

1. Initiating
2. Planning
3. Executing
4. Controlling
5. Closing

The practice of project management applies the five process groups within the three driving forces behind projects: time, resources and scope. This triple constraint, as shown in Figure 1-1, requires the project manager to constantly balance competing demands in order to meet stakeholder expectations.

Part 2 of this book provides more details on the five process groups of project management. A solid foundation of the generally accepted principles of each process group will be explained within the planning profession context.

It is important to emphasize once again that project management can be used in many forms. On one end of the scale is the way the National Aeronautics and Space Administration (NASA) applies the project management process in launching the space shuttle. Each launch involves thousands of people, millions of dollars, a very tight schedule and a hugely complex series of tasks to produce a successful launch and mission. There is very little room for error and the consequences of any errors can be catastrophic. The only way that NASA can confidently approach the launch of the space shuttle is by applying project management processes and principles; to do otherwise would invite disaster.

A contrast with the space shuttle might be the preparation of a local zoning ordinance. The consequences of missing a deadline or not performing a task in the drafting of a zoning ordinance may not be as dramatic and serious as with the space shuttle; however, they are still unacceptable and often avoidable. The principles and processes of project management can be applied to the preparation of a zoning ordinance—just as they are applied to the launching of the space shuttle—to bring the project in on time, within budget and of high quality.

Project management applies to planners just as much as it applies to the space industry, construction field and IT environment. Much of the planner's job is oriented towards producing a quality plan within time and resource constraints. This book provides a methodology for doing just that.

REVIEW

- Drastic times call for drastic measures.

- Bringing quality planning projects in on time and within budget is no longer a luxury—it is a necessity.

- Project management offers a way to meet increasing demands being placed on planners.

- Planners have the skills to be excellent project managers.

- Planners are not the only ones who can benefit from project management.

- Project management is not just another management fad.

- Many types of organizations can use the project management techniques in many different ways; it is not a cookie-cutter approach.

- Project management consists of five process groups: Initiating, Planning, Executing, Controlling and Closing.

- This book provides a hands-on, real-world approach to the planner on how to apply project management practices and principles to the planning environment.

RESOURCES

Drucker, Peter F. *The New Realities: In Government and Politics/In Economics and Business/In Society and World View.* New York, NY: Harper & Row, 1989.

Kerzner, Harold. *Project Management: A Systems Approach to Planning, Scheduling, and Controlling, 6th Ed.* New York: NY: John Wiley & Sons, Inc., 1998.

Project Management Institute, Inc. *A Guide to the Project Management Body of Knowledge (PMBOK® Guide), 2000 Edition.* Newtown Square, PA: Project Management Institute, Inc., 2000. All rights reserved. Materials from this publication have been reproduced with the permission of PMI. Unauthorized reproduction of this material is strictly prohibited.

Project Management Institute, Inc. *A Framework for Project Management, Participant's Manual,* Newtown Square, PA: Project Management Institute, Inc., 1999.

To Managers and Supervisors

In helping others to succeed we insure our own success.

—WILLIAM FEATHER

The person who knows "how" will always have a job. The person who knows "why" will always be his boss.

—DIANE RAVITCH

Someone once defined the manager, only half in jest, as that person who sees the visitors so that everyone else can get the work done.

—H. MINTZBERG

INTRODUCTION

This chapter is written to the managers and supervisors in the organization. Managers and supervisors are charged with meeting the needs and expectations of their superiors in a way that does not demoralize or burn out their staff. Add to this the constantly shifting and unpredictable nature of working in a political environment, and the job of being a planning manager becomes extremely difficult.

The most important measuring stick for a manager, though, is production. If a manager is not able to rally his/her troops to produce quality work products in a timely and effective manner, that manager will not be a manager for long. The success of a manager is only as long as the last deliverable. It really does not matter how much a manager has produced in the past or how impressive their plans are. If the manager does not constantly produce tangible work products that meet or exceed the expectations of the customers, they will soon be looking for employment elsewhere.

While the loss of employment would not be a fun thing for a manager to go through, the inability to meet his/her own professional goals and expectations would be even more devastating. The planning manager is driven to not only meet the expectations of their bosses and the community, they are driven to meet their own goals and expectations. This usually involves effecting positive change in the community.

PLANNING STAFF ARE SELF-MOTIVATORS

Why do people enter the planning profession? Why are we motivated to tolerate the long hours, mediocre pay and unreal expectations? Why do we put up with endless public meetings and the occasional two-faced politician? It's very simple: we want to do the right thing. We are motivated by a deep drive to make our neighborhoods and communities a better place in which to live. These motivations, while possibly covered over by years of bad coffee and scrambled public address systems, are still at the heart of the drive behind planning managers.

These comments may come across as a little sappy; however, it is important to remember why we entered the planning profession so that we can focus that energy into our role as a planning manager.

To help do that, let me tell you a personal story. I was a manager of about 30 multidisciplinary professionals in a large water management agency. I had four supervisors from four different professional backgrounds reporting to me. One of the supervisors had a PhD in biology and supervised a group of environmental scientists working on long-range water quality plans. Samantha (not her real name) was an intelligent and talented individual, who also happened to be married to an American Institute of Certified Planners member.

One day, Samantha came into my office and asked if she could attend (with her husband) the next national American Planning Association (APA) conference, and focus her attention on the sessions dealing with environmental and water issues. I approved her travel and asked her to give a summary of the conference at our next staff meeting. She agreed and went to the conference.

An amazing thing happened. At our next staff meeting, Samantha gave the most impassioned summary of an APA conference that I have ever heard. It made me want to jump up and immediately register for next year's conference. She told of a group of bright, motivated individuals from all backgrounds trying to do the right thing. She was amazed at the racial and gender diversity of the conference attendees and how open they were to learning from each other. She was also amazed at the variety and complexity of the topics covered in the conference sessions. Samantha had no idea that planners were so vibrant, open and involved in their work. (She had been married to one for years!)

Sometimes we take for granted what we, as planners, are trying to accomplish and how we are trying to accomplish it. We overlook, or cover over, our motives that originally brought us into the profession. It often takes a fresh perspective of someone who comes from a totally different background to tell us how impressed they are with planners and how proud they feel to work with us. Samantha was "hooked" on planning after that APA conference, and her infectious review of the conference hooked others and reminded me of what a valued role we play.

As planning managers, we especially cannot forget what originally brought us into the profession and what keeps us here. This is the greatest motivational tool we have for our staff and ourselves.

BEYOND MOTIVATION

However, motivation is not enough. We must provide our staff with the tools and the organization for them to do their jobs at a higher level and in a more professional manner. As managers, we must feel confident enough to do one of the most difficult things any manager can do: back off and let our staff do their job. Provide the tools, framework and techniques for our staff to be productive and successful, and then turn them loose. Remember Samantha, and remember that we have the luxury of managing highly motivated individuals. Planners—almost to a fault— want to do the right thing by doing the job right. Let's give them the tools they need to effectively apply their motivation and then get out of the way.

Our organizations are usually not arranged to let people most effectively do their jobs. Typically, organizations are designed around the assumptions that employees are inept and could not find their way out of a broom closet without the help of a manager. This is absurd and must be thrown out of the highest level office. Most organizations (with planning organizations being no exception) are hierarchical in nature. For any decision to be made, it must first go though about seven thou-

Figure 2-1. Hierarchical Organizational Structure

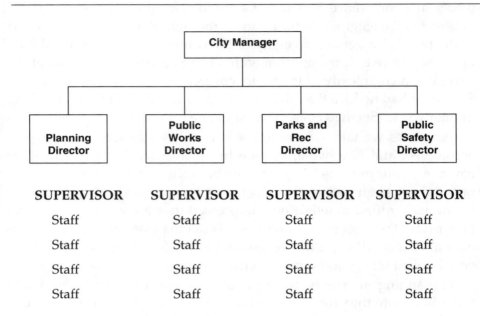

sand organizational layers with an accompanying form to be signed off by each layer. It is a system built on mistrust and a "Cover Your Assets" mentality that breeds cynicism almost as fast as it builds bureaucracy.

As absurd and insane as these organizational structures may be, they are here to stay—at least for a while. Our job as planning managers is to not let the organizational structure get in the way of producing results. How do we do that?

We basically build a better mousetrap using project management. Let's take a look at the organizational structure for a typical organization. Figure 2-1 portrays an average hierarchical arrangement.

As you can see, the organization in Figure 2-1 is divided into several functional areas. These are sometimes called "smokestacks" because they rise vertically through the organization. A functional area might be engineering, public works, planning and zoning or environmental sciences. Line managers oversee the functional segments of the organization. Typically, the line managers have a similar technical background as the folks who report to them. Frequently, the line manager was promoted to management because he/she exhibited excellent technical skills and abilities in their respective field. They were generally not promoted to management positions because they showed strong and competent management skills.

Management is often the only logical next step up in an organization for a technically competent individual. Most organizations do not have technical career tracks that parallel management tracks; once an employee peaks in their technical job area, the only next step for a promotion is into management.

Line managers are responsible for completing tasks or projects that are directly related to their profession. If an employee in the public works department is asked to contribute part of his/her time putting together public water demands for a comprehensive plan, they must first get authorization from their manager to spend time on the task of developing public water demands. The organizational structure is not designed to easily accommodate projects that require tasks performed by staff outside of their immediate area of influence.

The typical current form of organizational structure dates back hundreds of years to military commands. In those kinds of organizations, hierarchical, "command and control" organizational forms made sense and saved lives. It was unacceptable to break ranks and begin fighting independently in someone else's battle. Lives could be lost unnecessarily if the troops did not limit their activities to only those authorized by their superiors.

In today's fast-changing and increasingly demanding work environment, the old military-based form of operation does not make sense. In fact, it can do a great deal of harm if followed religiously. Today's organizations and work units must be flexible and product-focused. They must be able to respond to new and changing demands, and contribute when and where the need arises.

While most planning organizations—and the organizations within which planning units operate—will never truly be organized around projects, we can make relatively minor changes to accommodate a project-driven environment. A matrix type of organizational structure may be the answer in many organizations. As Figure 2-2 shows, the strong matrix organization includes a mix of the traditional functional breakout and a project-driven form.

In a strong matrix organization, one of the "smokestacks" is a group of project managers. The project managers recruit staff from the other functional areas to work on their projects. For example, a project manager may be responsible for drafting a new zoning ordinance. The

Figure 2-2. Strong Matrix Organization

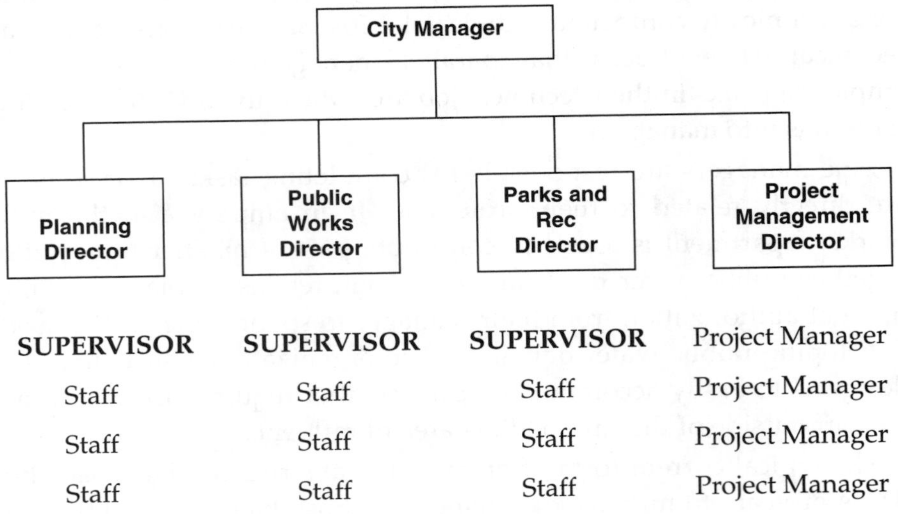

City Manager			
Planning Director	Public Works Director	Parks and Rec Director	Project Management Director
SUPERVISOR	**SUPERVISOR**	**SUPERVISOR**	Project Manager
Staff	Staff	Staff	Project Manager
Staff	Staff	Staff	Project Manager
Staff	Staff	Staff	Project Manager

project manager recruits an engineer from the public works department to assist in drafting setback requirements to accommodate public utilities. The project manager may also request that a staff member from the public safety department be on the project team to prepare and review the zoning code sections that relate to the safe design of cul-de-sacs in neighborhoods to accommodate emergency vehicles.

The concept of the project management group in the matrix environment is that the project manager in that section is only responsible for the successful completion of their project. Their primary focus is to get a quality project completed on time and within budget. The strengths and weaknesses of traditional organizational structures, matrix forms and project forms of organizations are presented in Table 2-1.

As stated earlier, most organizations are organized in the traditional hierarchical form. Functional areas are managed by functional managers. This can be a very efficient way to operate. There are clear lines of authority and in-line communication. Planners talk to planners, engineers talk to engineers, and so forth. Professional recognition is easier because the manager of a group usually has the same professional background as the people he/she manages. This allows for an appreciation of the technical skills of their profession and a familiarity with career paths.

Table 2-1. Strengths and Weaknesses of Organizational Structures

Organizational Structure	Strengths	Weaknesses
Functional/ Hierarchical	• Clear line of authority • Professional recognition • Familiar to most people	• Not conducive to projects and teams • Difficult to communicate across functional units • Project manager has little authority
Matrix	• Maintains familiar line of command structure • Addresses cross-functional needs of projects • Recognizes importance of projects	• Potentially confusing lines of communication • Middle managers have control over resources • Project authority can be divided
Projectized	• Designed to handle projects • Defines clear lines of authority for projects • Recognizes importance of project managers	• Unfamiliar to many • Temporary nature can be disruptive to staff • Professional development and coaching can be minimized

However, the traditional functional organization has a difficult time dealing with projects that require cross-functional teams. If a project requires a multidisciplinary team of professionals, a functional/hierarchical form of organization does not lend itself well to successful project completion. Functional managers are reluctant to allow staff from their organizational unit to work on a project managed by someone outside of their line of command. The functional manager loses control of his/her staff and control budgets. The functional manager is put in a very uncomfortable position.

The primary reason functional managers are reluctant to freely allow staff from their work units to work on projects outside of their control is that, in most organizations, they can only be harmed. If a functional manager agrees to let one of their staff temporarily work on a project managed by someone in another work unit, that functional manager still has all of their normal workload with fewer people to do the work. Their bosses still have the same expectations of them and will not be happy if the work under their control is not completed on time. There can be negative consequences to a line manager for letting their staff work on a project for which they are not responsible.

On the other hand, if the project to which their staff member has been temporarily assigned is successful, the lending functional manager does not get credit or recognition for the success. The project manager and the project manager's boss get credit for the success, not the manager that supplied the team member.

Most of the long-term projects that planners manage are multidisciplinary in nature and require project team members from various parts of the organization. The preparation of comprehensive plans is a classic example of the kind of project that is extremely difficult to manage in a traditional hierarchical organizational structure.

This brings us to the matrix form of organization. While it is not a panacea for all problems, it does offer some relief from the problems that plague the functional organization. In essence, the matrix organization pulls project managers from the hierarchical ranks of the organization and puts them in a separate "smokestack." By doing so, the organization is saying that the project managers and the projects they manage are of equal importance to the other functional units. It provides the project manager with an easier job of negotiating for team members because they now have the credibility of a line manager. This is extremely important for a project manager. In a strong matrix arrangement, a group of project managers is under a manager of project managers.

For comparison purposes, a brief discussion of a "projectized" organizational structure is in order. The projectized organizational structure is represented in Figure 2-3. A projectized organization is one that is organized around projects and project managers. Project managers are the equivalent in this type of organization to functional managers in a traditional organization. Their projects determine where staff fit in the structure. It is important to note that, since projects are by definition temporary, the projectized organization is usually in a fluid state. It is never cast in concrete. As projects are started and completed, the structure of the organization will change.

THE IMPORTANCE TO PLANNING MANAGERS

Why spend so much time talking about organizational structures to a bunch of planning managers? As I stated earlier, we as planners are ideally suited to a project-focused form of work. We think of the "big picture" and are inclusive not only in our work, but also in the way we approach our work. As a rule, we enjoy and encourage a wide range of participation in the development of our projects. We do this because we know that the final product benefits from diverse involvement. We also know that the more people and sets of eyes we involve in the develop-

Figure 2-3. Projectized Organization

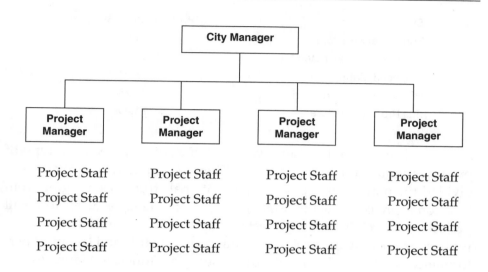

ment of a project, the better the final product will be. It is in our nature. It's the way we approach the world.

However, we sometimes fall short in the execution of our work. We bring a tremendous amount of technical skills, an inclusive attitude and a high degree of enthusiasm to our jobs and projects. In addition to these strong characteristics, we can benefit from a structured approach to accomplishing our goals.

Planning managers have the tremendous responsibility of trying to bring some strategic direction, focus and structure to people and organizations that are generally not completely in line with a planner's perspective. Understanding some of the reasons why we, on occasion, do not meet expectations can go a long way towards arriving at solutions. Knowing that the work we do as planners requires us to cross traditional organizational lines makes us more prepared when faced with challenging deadlines. Recognizing that most of our organizations are built upon a traditional/hierarchical form can help us understand how we might make recommendations for approaching projects using a matrix form. Being able to explain this concept to fellow managers and decision-makers can go a long way towards bringing planning projects to successful completion.

A study done by Erik Larson and David Gobeli of Oregon State University in the mid-1980s arrived at some startling conclusions. Larson

Figure 2-4. Project Success by Organizational Structure

Structure	Probability of Success
Functional Structure	34.0%
Functionally Dominated Matrix	34.4%
Balanced Matrix	55.9%
Project-Dominated Matrix	70.7%
Full Project Structure	71.4%

and Gobeli wondered if there was a relationship between the type of project organization and its success. They looked at 1,400 projects and divided them into five types of organizational structures, ranging from functional project structures using no project manager at all to a full project structure giving the project manager complete authority. Success was determined by the project meeting cost, schedule and technical performance objectives. The results of the study are found in Figure 2-4.

It is obvious from this study that, as an organization moves from a functional structure (which gives the project manager little or no

The Oregon Example

The Program. The State of Oregon has established the Oregon Project Management Certification Program (OPMCP). The objective of the program is to "produce successful state projects." The state has decided that using the project management way of doing business is the best way to achieve their objective. The program is offered through the Department of Administrative Services (DAS) and is open to all state and local government employees. It is a concerted effort between the DAS, other state agencies and the Chemeketa Community College. "With the complexity of work increasing, our time to complete projects decreasing, and public expectations rising, projects are and will be key to our future success." (OPMCP Web site)

Two Levels of Certification. The program offers two levels of certification: (1) Oregon Project Management Associate, which is achieved by completing a series of courses and passing a knowledge base test; and (2) Oregon State Project Manager, which is granted after taking a series of courses and passing the Project Management Professional exam offered through PMI.

authority of his/her project) to an organizational structure that gives the project manager more authority, the probability of the project being successful dramatically increases. As the project manager is given more authority, the chances for success improve.

LET GO!

Having been a manager for many years, I know how difficult it can be to stand back and let an employee do their job. It sounds so simple and so right, yet it is quite difficult. We take great pains to hire just the right person, provide them with computers and other equipment worth thousands of dollars, and pay them decent wages and benefits, yet when it comes to delegating work and letting them do their job, we fall short. We instinctively feel that they need our regular oversight and guidance; in reality, all they need for us to do is let them do their job.

Letting go is hard to do, yet the results are obvious. When managers and supervisors provide their project managers with the right tools and resources, and let them do their job, the projects are successful. If the organization can be permanently (or even temporarily) arranged to accommodate the project manager and their team, the chances for success skyrocket. As managers, we have to remember what we are ultimately trying to do: successfully complete a quality project on time and within budget. This does not mean that it has to have our fingerprints all over it to shine. In fact, there is the possibility that the project will be better than we could have ever imagined, but we will never know until we back off, get out of the way and let the project manager do their job.

REVIEW

- Planning managers and supervisors are charged with meeting the needs and expectations of their superiors and the public in a way that does not demoralize or burn out their staff.
- A planning manager must constantly produce tangible work products that meet or exceed the expectations of their customers.
- Planning managers and supervisors must give their staff the tools to do their jobs well.
- Planning staff are self-motivated and want to do the right thing.
- Our organizations are not always arranged to help managers delegate effectively.
- Hierarchical organizational structures do not lend themselves well to successful project management.

- Organizations and managers that allow their project managers to do their job have a much better chance of being successful.
- Planning managers and supervisors must learn to let go and let their staff do their job.

RESOURCES

Bennis, Warren. *On Becoming a Leader*. Reading, MA: Addison-Wesley, 1989.

Bennis, Warren and Burt Nanus. *Leaders: The Strategies for Taking Charge*. New York, NY: Harper & Row, 1985.

Frame, J. Davidson. *Managing Projects in Organizations*. San Francisco, CA: Jossey-Bass, 1995.

Larson, Erik and David Gobeli. "The Barriers Affecting Project Success," Project Management Institute, Inc. *Measuring Success: Proceedings of the 17th Annual Seminars & Symposium*, Montreal, Canada, 1986.

Project Management Institute, Inc. Web site: http://www.pmi.org

The Oregon Project Management Certification Program. Web site: http://training.das.state.or.us/steps/opmcp.htm

Zaleznik, Abraham. *The Managerial Mystique: Restoring Leadership in Business*. New York, NY: Harper & Row, 1989.

The Process of Project Management for Planners

In Part 2 of this book, we explore the five processes of project management: Chapter 3, Initiating; Chapter 4, Planning; Chapter 5, Executing; Chapter 6, Controlling; and Chapter 7, Closing. The titles of the five processes are consistent with the PMBOK® Guide; however, the five chapters are written for planners. Planning examples are used and the processes of project management have been placed in the context of planning.

Each of the five chapters in Part 2 begins with an interview with a fictional planner. The interviews highlight each chapter's subject and introduce the concepts that are further explored in the text. Following the main body of each chapter is a brief review of the key points, job aids to bring back to the workplace, and resources identifying referenced sources and additional information the reader can consult.

3

Initiating

The first step is the hardest.

—MADAME DE VICHY-DEFFAND

The secret of getting ahead is getting started. The secret of getting started is breaking your complex overwhelming tasks into small manageable tasks, and then starting on the first one.

—MARK TWAIN

They laughed at Joan of Arc, but she went right ahead and built it.

—GRACIE ALLEN

INTERVIEW

Following is an interview with the planning director of a medium-sized city in the Midwest. Her name is Betty Skehan and she has been planning director for nearly 10 years.

Project Management for Planners (PMfP): Betty, what do you think is the most important part of starting a project?

Betty: Without a doubt, the most important part of starting a project is beginning on the right foot.

PMfP: What do you mean by that?

Betty: For a project to be started properly, some basic questions need to be asked. Don't laugh when I say this, but one of the most important questions to ask is, "What is the project?" It may seem like an obvious answer at first, but if some thought isn't given up front to accurately identify the project, your project will be doomed from the start. It is absolutely critical that the project has proper limitations, and not be something that just keeps going and going, with no end in sight.

PMfP: You're right. At first, the answer seems pretty obvious, but we do see on occasion a project that just doesn't seem to want to die.

Betty: Absolutely! Those kinds of projects were usually never given clear boundaries and definitions. As a result, deadlines are missed and budgets are blown. It's not a pretty sight.

PMfP: What other kinds of issues related to initiating a project must a planner be particularly aware of?

Betty: Two things. First, picking the right project manager. Not everyone should be a project manager. One of the most difficult decisions I ever made as planning director was to not choose an excellent employee to be a project manager for an important and visible project. Not all planners are created equal and not all planners should be project managers. In general, don't pick a project manager solely based upon technical expertise. Just because a transportation planner is the best computer modeler you have for determining levels of service, he/she should not be automatically chosen to be the project manager for preparing the metropolitan planning organization's long-range traffic improvement plan. The project manager must have skills other than just technical. One of the worst things we can do for an employee and a project is to put the wrong person in charge.

PMfP: What is the other important issue related to project management for planners to be aware of?

Betty: Without a doubt, it is accurately identifying the stakeholders of planning projects. As planners, we tend to take this task for granted and, in doing so, overlook some critically important stakeholders. Planning projects are incredibly complex, involving all kinds of people, institutions and interests. Before we begin work on the actual project, it is extremely important that we go through the process of identifying the stakeholders.

PMfP: Thanks for your insight, Betty. We appreciate the key points you have made for our readers.

Betty: You're welcome. Always glad to help fellow planners.

INITIATING

As Betty said in the interview, one of the most important parts of any project is getting started on the right foot, and that begins with properly defining the project. It is estimated that approximately 5% of the project

Table 3-1. How a Project Manager Spends Time

Process Group	Percent of Project Manager's Time
Initiating	5%
Planning	35%
Executing	25%
Controlling	25%
Closing	10%

manager's time should be spent on the Initiating process (see Table 3-1). There are several different ways to define a project. The simplest and quickest way to start is by creating a project scope statement.

Project Scope Statement

The project scope statement must be in writing and does not need to be lengthy. It is intended to be a simple statement of the purpose of the project and a brief overview of the final product (or deliverable). It is a relatively short document (ranging in total length from a few paragraphs to no more than two pages) and should answer the following three basic questions:

1. Why is the project being done?
2. What are the primary project objectives?
3. What will be the final product (or deliverable)?

Prior to the preparation of the project scope statement, hundreds of assumptions have been made about the final product. Everyone who has spoken about the project has their own unique understanding of what it should contain. Most likely, the project manager has a completely different perception of the final product than everyone else. This is a recipe for disaster.

The last thing you want to do is to bring the first draft of a comprehensive plan to your planning commission in a public meeting and have the members stare back at you in disbelief and horror. It is critical to get the basics of the project in writing before any work on the project begins. Our first instinct is to begin preparing the final product before a common understanding of the simplest parameters have been stated and agreed upon.

What is a Project? When preparing the scope statement, it is a good idea to use the PMI's definition of a project. PMI's *PMBOK® Guide* states that "a project is a temporary endeavor undertaken to create a unique product or service." (PMI, 2000, p. 4)

A couple of points need to be made about the definition of a project. First, it is temporary. This may seem obvious at first, but very often this concept is lost in the middle of a project. For a project to truly be a project, it must have a beginning and an end. If a "project" does not have a beginning and an end, it is a "process."

Second, a project results in a unique product, service or outcome. For planning projects, this is pretty obvious. Every comprehensive plan, zoning code or site plan is unique. The primary steps in preparing planning products may be similar, but the final products are uniquely different. Therefore, the process of producing them involves project management.

Shop It Around. Present the project scope statement to as many people and decision-making bodies as soon as possible. The more people that see and understand the project scope statement early on, the better your chances of project success. It is consistent with human nature that if a person has an opportunity to review and participate in the development of a project, the more likely they will accept the final product. That is especially true for the project scope statement. The earlier the project manager can get input and involvement by affected parties on the design of the project, the greater the chances for triumph.

Job Aid 3-1 is provided to help in the preparation and review of the project scope statement. It is a checklist that includes the major stakeholders to involve in the preparation of the project scope statement.

Identification of Stakeholders

Identification of stakeholders is a key component of initiating a project that can easily define success or failure. This is especially true for planning projects. Planning projects typically involve a wide range of special interests and decision-makers. For the project to be successful, the appropriate affected parties must participate in the development of the project.

Figure 3-1 provides a helpful way to organize stakeholders and decide the best use of the project manager's time. Not all stakeholders are created equal. In fact, in a complex project, many of the stakeholders should not require a great deal of time of the project manager and team. The purpose of Figure 3-1 is to identify those stakeholders who have a

Figure 3-1. Stakeholder Matrix

	Quadrant III High Amenability to Reason Low Ability to Influence	Quadrant I High Amenability to Reason High Ability to Influence
	Quadrant IV Low Amenability to Reason Low Ability to Influence	Quadrant II Low Amenability to Reason High Ability to Influence

Amenability to Reason (vertical axis, L to H)

Ability to Influence (horizontal axis, L to H)

high ability to influence the project and are amenable to reason. These stakeholders are represented in Quadrant I of Figure 3-1.

Stakeholders represented in Quadrant I are both powerful and amenable to reason. The project manager and team should focus most of their time with the stakeholders in Quadrant I.

The project manager and team should go through a brainstorming session to: (1) identify all stakeholders; and (2) place all stakeholders in the appropriate quadrant.

This is an excellent exercise to identify and assess all stakeholders. It is also a good team-building exercise for the project manager and their team. Going through the process of identifying and categorizing stakeholders with the project team will ensure that all appropriate stakeholders are identified. This information will become more valuable as the project progresses.

Once the Quadrant I stakeholders have been identified, the specific needs of the stakeholders can then be specified. For example, if the project involves developing the site plan for a new subdivision, different stakeholders in Quadrant I will want to be involved differently. The surrounding neighborhood association would definitely be a Quadrant I stakeholder. They have a high ability to influence the project and, if properly handled, have a high amenability to reason.

The local government engineering department will have a different set of needs. They are another example of a Quadrant I stakeholder because they have a high ability to influence the project and are amenable to reason. The degree to which an engineering department is amenable to reason may be open for debate; however, their main job is to ensure that the public's health, safety and welfare are protected through

Table 3-2. Quadrant I Stakeholder Information Needs

Stakeholder Needs	Neighborhood Association	Engineering Department
Status Reports	Needed	Needed
Schedules of Future Activities	Needed	Not Needed
Project Budget	Needed	Not Needed
Copies of Subcontractor Specifications	Not Needed	Needed
Notices of Public Meetings	Needed	Not Needed
Overall Engineering Specifications	Needed	Needed
Press Releases	Needed	Not Needed
Accident and Safety Records	Not Needed	Needed
Construction Timeline	Needed	Needed

adherence to the local codes. As long as the codes are met, the engineering folks are satisfied.

Table 3-2 presents a partial list of the types of information and involvement that Quadrant I stakeholders may want and how those needs can differ depending on the stakeholder. Table 3-2 uses the example of the local neighborhood association and the local government engineering department. This table is intended to make a point. The determination on "Needed" and "Not Needed" must be made on an individual project basis.

A couple of points become obvious when looking at Table 3-2:

- Not all stakeholders are created equal.
- Not all stakeholders have the same needs.

In this example, both parties need engineering specs; however, how those specs will be used will differ. The neighborhood association will be looking at the specs to see what specific impacts may occur to their surrounding homes, while the engineering department will determine if the specs meet code. Therefore, even when stakeholders have the same information needs, their use of the information may be dramatically different.

Deliverables

The next major step in the Initiating process of a planning project is the identification of the project's major deliverables. The major deliverables are the "must-have" products coming out of the project. In other words, the project would be considered a failure if these products were not produced.

The best way to identify the project deliverables is to base them on the needs and expectations of the stakeholders. The previous section of this chapter outlined the process of identifying stakeholders and understanding why they are stakeholders. If the project is to be successful, it is especially important that the most important stakeholder expectations and needs be met.

Job Aid 3-2 provides a good basis to begin identifying the major project deliverables based upon the expectations of the stakeholders. For example, in order for the city manager to consider a new comprehensive plan for the city to be acceptable, it must contain a capital improvement component describing the costs and funding sources of implementing the plan. It is critical that the project manager identify early on that the plan must contain a capital improvement element for the project (in this example, the development of a new comprehensive plan) to be successful.

Resource Requirements

An estimate of the resources needed to complete a project must be included in the Initiating process of a project. At this stage, it is recognized that the estimates will be approximate. However, it is important to arrive at rough estimates of the human and financial capital that will be needed to complete the project. More detailed calculations of the resources required to complete the project will be prepared in the next process (see Chapter 4, *Planning*). The estimates figured at this point will be used to determine a "go" or "no go" decision on the project.

People. In determining a rough estimate of the human resource requirements of a planning project, it is important to highlight a couple of points. The first is the importance of diversity. Planning projects must meet a high standard of excellence and acceptance. Taxpayers and elected officials demand that planning projects be representative of the community and that they meet the needs of a wide range of constituents. The best way to meet these high standards is to have a diverse project team.

Diversity is measured in several ways. Following is a brief list of diversity characteristics that should be addressed in determining the team for a planning project.

• *Race and ethnicity.* As stated earlier, planning projects require a diverse perspective to meet the needs of a community. The racial and ethnic characteristics of a project team should be representative of the community being planned. It is simply unacceptable to have a project team that does not reflect the local community. All efforts should be made to represent the racial and ethnic makeup of the community on the project team.

• *Gender.* The communities for which we plan include males and females. Make sure that the team preparing the plan includes this mix. Males and females bring a unique perspective to a project and, for a planning project to be successful, both perspectives must be represented on the team.

• *Profession.* It is easy to slip into a planning-centric perspective. Sometimes, as planners, we are our own worst enemies. Recognize that other professions have something important to say and include them on the team. Engineers, geologists, economists and environmental scientists make a team stronger. If their expertise is needed on the project, make sure they are included in the team.

• *Personality.* The worst thing a project manager can do is to develop a project team made up of people with the same view of the world. Introverts and extroverts, sensors and feelers, and perceivers and judgers all bring a unique and valuable perspective to a project team. Don't be intimidated by a mix of personality types. Diversity builds strengths, not weaknesses.

The second major point to note when discussing the human resource requirements of a project is justification and roles. When determining the general requirements for the team, be sure to include a brief description of why that person or group of people is required. Clearly understand and be able to articulate the role each team member will play on a team. The best way to do that is to relate each project team member to the final deliverable. In other words, be able to explain how the final product will be improved by the inclusion of each team member.

Clearly tying the requirements to the deliverables will avoid later criticism by staff and managers in the organization of empire-building or overstaffing a project. If an honest relationship cannot be made between a team member and the project deliverables, then do not ask for the team member. It will only harm the project manager's credibility later on.

Money. At the Initiating stage of a project, it is important for decision-makers to know project cost estimates. More detailed cost estimates will be produced later; however, rough estimates should be made at this point.

Things to consider when estimating preliminary costs are:

- *Personnel.* How many people are needed? For how long and at what rate of pay?

- *Equipment.* What kind of equipment will be needed? Will it need to be leased or bought and at what rate? Make sure that a rough estimate of maintenance costs is included. Equipment can include office equipment (computers and digitizers) as well as construction equipment (bulldozers and dump trucks).

- *Materials.* Will there be substantial costs of materials such as graphics? Remember: at this stage, we are only considering major expenses associated with the project. Planning projects generally do not have large material costs; however, consider the question at this stage.

- *Overhead.* All projects require some sort of overhead associated with people, equipment and materials. The most obvious overhead expense includes items such as utilities and office space insurance.

Job Aid 3-3 provides a worksheet that can be used to estimate general project costs. The audience for this information will be decision-makers who will want to know the magnitude of the project costs. Detailed costs will be provided later in the project. At the Initiating stage, enough information to decide a "go" or "no go" choice is all that is needed.

Organization of the Project

How the project is organized will greatly influence the project's chances of success. The project must be organized in a way that is most effective in producing results and that reflects the organizational context of the surroundings.

Effectiveness. In an ideal world, the project would be organized in a "projectized" structure. The project manager would be the lead and all team members would report to the project manager. The primary responsibility of the team members would be the success of the project and most, if not all, of their time would be spent on the project. Figure 2-3 (in Chapter 2) shows what a projectized organizational structure would look like.

Context. In all likelihood, project managers of planning projects will not be operating in a projectized organizational structure. It is not reasonable to expect that the makeup of a local government—or even a consulting firm—will be restructured to reflect large planning projects being undertaken. Traditional line management organizational structures are most common and within which planning project managers most often operate. As a result, the project's organization must reflect this fact.

The organization of the project will be set up around the context of the "parent" organization. When setting up the organization of the project, the project manager must recognize that the project team members come from another part of the organization. Another point especially important to remember is that the project organizational structure must acknowledge that the team members report to a supervisor or manager outside the realm of the project manager when operating in a matrix environment. This will alleviate a lot of concerns from the line managers and supervisors later on.

When putting together the project organization, the following steps should be taken:

- Identify the major deliverables that will come from the project.
- Associate one key person to lead the preparation of each major deliverable (task manager).
- Determine which staff will work under the key deliverable task managers.
- Speak first to the line manager of the proposed task manager and task staff to request their time on the project.
- Speak with the task managers and staff about working on the project.

After speaking with the appropriate managers and staff, put the general project organizational structure on paper, using one of the styles discussed earlier in this book. Choose the structure that best suits the existing culture of the current organization and that represents the project.

Preparing a Project Charter

The Project Charter is a single document that outlines the basic requirements and expectations of a project. The purpose of the Project Charter is to get management support for the use of resources for a particular project. A good Project Charter makes sure that key managers and decision-makers understand the purpose of the project and what will be required from the organization to produce the project deliverables.

Job Aid 3-4 presents a template for a Project Charter. It is based on a model Project Charter that was prepared for the South Florida Water Management District (the District). The District is beginning to implement the Comprehensive Everglades Restoration Plan (CERP) to restore the health and productivity of the Everglades. The CERP consists of 68 components that, when complete, will implement the plan objectives. In order to provide some consistency in how the projects were organized, the District developed a template for Project Charters. "Case Study #1: Saving the Everglades" (Chapter 8) includes a detailed description of the CERP.

The major components of a Project Charter include:

- *Project Title* (the title of the specific project)
- *Project Sponsor* (a senior manager within the organization that promotes and explains the project to other managers)
- *Project Management Oversight Team* (a group of managers within the organization that are provided with periodic updates on the project's status)
- *Project Manager* (the name of the project manager)
- *Project Team* (names of the key project team members)
- *Project Location* (the geographic location of the project)
- *Project Description* (outlines the project objectives and deliverables)
- *Justification* (summarizes the stakeholders and their expectations for the project)
- *Preliminary Methodology* (briefly describes how the project will be performed)
- *Business Areas Involved* (a good place to provide the project organization and describe from where the key staff will come)
- *Estimated Costs/Resources* (described earlier in this chapter)
- *Assumptions* (briefly describes what factors are considered to be true, real or certain for the project to be a success)
- *Constraints* (all projects exist within the context of time, resources, staffing, physical, political and environmental constraints)
- *Roles and Responsibilities* (roles and responsibilities of the project sponsor, project management oversight team, project manager, and the project team and support staff)

REVIEW

- Initiating is the first process of project management.
- Initiating consists of several components and steps.
- The project scope statement identifies the project purpose, products/deliverables and primary objectives.
- The process of identifying stakeholders clarifies the project expectations that will define success or failure for planning projects.
- A project must produce deliverables that need to be identified during the Initiating process.
- Resources required to complete the project are generally identified during the Initiating process, including people and financial resources.
- How the project is organized within the context of the "parent" organization will define how team members and their line managers will operate.
- The Project Charter rolls up all of the pertinent project information into one document that allows senior managers and decision-makers within the organization to make an informed decision about whether or not to support the project.

Job Aid 3-1. Project Scope Statement Review Checklist

Person or Organization Reviewing Scope Statement	Date Reviewed	Primary Presenter	Required Follow-up
Planning Director			
City/County Manager			
Planning Commission			
City Council/ County Commissioners			
Community/Citizen Groups			

Job Aid 3-2. Identifying Project Deliverables

Stakeholder	Stakeholder Expectations	Project Deliverable
Elected Officials		
City/County Manager		
Neighborhood Associations		
Local Business Community		
Regional/State Reviewing Agencies		
Others:		

Job Aid 3-3. Project Cost Estimation Worksheet

Cost Factor	Quantity	Duration	Rate	Cost Estimate
Personnel				
Equipment				
Materials				
Overhead				

Job Aid 3-4. Project Charter Template

SOUTH FLORIDA WATER MANAGEMENT DISTRICT

Project Charter

> The project charter is a document that authorizes the manager to apply organizational resources to project activities, and to proceed with finalizing the project scope and developing the project plan.

Project Title: [enter project title here]

Project Manager: [enter project manager name here]

Level of Empowerment: [modify this or add any specific authority the project charter is giving to the project manager, such as authority to approve|recommend expenditures of funds or assign|recommend human resources to staff the project]

This project charter has been initiated by the [initiating organization] and authorizes the project manager to expend [District|Department|Division] resources to complete a project plan for the [project title].

Approvals:

_____	_____
[sponsor]	Date
_____	_____
[oversight committee member]	Date
_____	_____
[oversight committee member]	Date
_____	_____
[oversight committee member]	Date

Project Title:

Project Sponsor: [name, title]

Project Management Oversight Team: [name(s), title(s)]

Project Manager: [name, title]

Job Aid 3-4. Project Charter Template (continued)

Project Team: [name(s), title(s)]

Project Location: [where the work will be carried out]

Project Description: [briefly describe the project objectives]

Justification: [include the business need the project will address and, if possible, tie it to the District's mission; identify any statutory or legislative requirements; include goals, objectives and performance measures; detail the benefits to the District]

Preliminary Methodology: [state the approach the project manager or team will take to develop the project plan]

Business Areas Involved: [organizational units, programs or functional areas]

Estimated Costs/Resources: [estimated cost, human and other resource requirements]

Assumptions: [factors that, for planning purposes, will be considered to be true, real or certain]

Constraints: [include time, resources, staff time in full-time equivalents, physical, political, environmental, etc.]

Roles and Responsibilities:

The project sponsor is responsible for:
- communicating District objectives
- overseeing cross-organizational participation
- providing a focal point to resolve issues escalated from the management oversight team

The management oversight team is responsible for:
- providing oversight and guidance to the project manager
- approving policies, plans, standards and procedures, including the quality assurance, implementation, risk management and performance measurement plans
- approving, as required, changes in project scope
- monitoring project progress and performance
- providing a focal point to resolve issues escalated from the project manager

The project manager is responsible for:
- the project's overall performance and success
- approving policies, processes and procedures developed by project team members
- being the focal point for communication between the project and management oversight
- escalating to the management oversight team issues that cannot be resolved at the project level
- developing and maintaining the project plan

The project team/support/coordinator are responsible for:
- developing strategies to deliver the project
- documenting, as required, project plan elements
- developing the project Work Breakdown Structure
- developing detailed schedules
- developing resource estimates

RESOURCES

Baker, Sunny and Kim Baker. *The Complete Idiot's Guide to Project Management, 2nd Ed.* Indianapolis, IN: Alpha Books, 2000.

Michael Greer Project Management. Web site:
http://www.michaelgreer.com

Project Management Institute, Inc. *A Guide to the Project Management Body of Knowledge (PMBOK® Guide), 2000 Edition.* Newtown Square, PA: Project Management Institute, Inc., 2000. All rights reserved. Materials from this publication have been reproduced with the permission of PMI. Unauthorized reproduction of this material is strictly prohibited.

4

Planning

I try to take one day at a time, but sometimes several days attack me at once.

—ASHLEIGH BRILLIANT

To do great important tasks, two things are necessary: a plan and not quite enough time.

—ANONYMOUS

Hard work is often the easy work you did not do at the proper time.

—BERNARD MELTZER

INTERVIEW

The following interview is with Charlie Newbert, Vice President in Charge of Planning for a large engineering and planning consulting firm.

PMfP: Why is it so important to spend a lot of time talking about planning a project with a bunch of planners? Shouldn't we know how to plan?

Charlie: As planners, we plan for communities, neighborhoods and regions. Usually our planning is defined by geography or place. Planning, as it relates to project management, is a different kind of beast.

PMfP: Isn't planning "planning"?

Charlie: There are some similarities, for sure. For example, project planning is future-focused like community planning. A desired end is defined and the best way to achieve that end is identified. A list of tasks and timelines is prepared. However, there are some differences.

PMfP: Such as?

Charlie: Project planning is totally focused on preparing the deliverable. In our case as planners, the deliverable is usually some kind of plan. That means that project planning outlines in detail how a community plan will be prepared. Deliverables are defined in detail, tasks are identified necessary to complete the deliverables, timelines are established and needed resources are specified.

PMfP: So, it's a plan for a plan?

Charlie: Sort of. Instead of calling it "a plan for a plan," I like to call it a detailed description of exactly who will perform tasks, when they will perform those tasks, and how much time and money they need to complete the tasks in order to prepare a quality deliverable on time and within budget.

PMfP: In other words, project planning requires a very detailed and specific identification of how the project—in our case, a community plan—will be completed?

Charlie: Exactly. It is a blueprint for preparing a community plan with tasks, responsibilities, timelines and allocated resources identified. As a private sector planner, I believe that the only way to prepare a quality community plan on time, and still make a profit, is to spend the time up front to prepare a thorough project plan.

PMfP: We really appreciate your time, Charlie. Thanks.

Charlie: I have enjoyed it.

PLANNING

It is estimated that the Planning process of project management should require approximately 35% of the project manager's time over the life of the project (see Table 3-1 in Chapter 3). Project planning requires the project manager to think through the project and remain focused on the end goal, which is the final deliverable. The deliverables dictate how the project proceeds from beginning to end.

This chapter is divided into several sections that describe the different aspects of planning a project. As with the other chapters in Part 2 of this book, this chapter is directed towards the planner as a project manager. As such, this chapter begins with a challenge to planners who are also project managers. As you will read, our chosen profession can offer some advantages—and obstacles—when it comes to being a project manager.

The Challenge to Planners

Planners should pay particular attention to the Planning process of project management for two main reasons. First, we have the skills needed to perform this process flawlessly. Our training and experience is centered on identifying end goals and determining how to best achieve those goals. The professional and personal tools that we have developed over the years are perfectly suited to performing the Planning process of project management. Since we do have the necessary basic skills to perform this process of project management, we must not assume that we automatically know how to do this type of planning. As a project manager, a planner must keep an open mind to planning a project. It is different than planning a community. It requires a different kind of vigilance.

This brings us to the second reason why planners must pay particular attention to the Planning process of project management. Planning a project requires a different set of planning skills than planning a community. While it is true that planning a project and planning a community do contain similar perspectives in some areas, they are markedly different in others. Planning a project can be a tedious effort with little recognition of its importance. As a planner, our plans are usually in the spotlight of the community or decision-makers. Our community planning work attracts attention and interest from many people and institutions. On the other hand, when planning a project, one of the most difficult things is to remain focused on the task when nobody else seems to care. In fact, our organizations tend to place time constraints and expectations that do not support proper project planning. They want to see immediate action on the project. Even fellow workers question why they need to spend so much time up front on a project before any of the "real work" can begin.

As planners planning a project instead of a community, we must recognize that, while our planning skills can be an asset, they can also be a liability. We must keep our minds open to a different kind of planning that demands a different perspective, and a lesser level of internal and external support.

Project Description

There are many ways to describe a project. In the previous chapter, we discussed how to describe a project at the Initiating process. In the Initiating process of a project, the project description is a fairly brief and

Key Points to Remember
When Writing a WBS

- Always keep the deliverable in mind.
- Start general and become more specific.
- Use the *verb + object* format.
- Keep statements short and to the point.
- Apply a consistent and simple numbering system.

- The size and complexity of a WBS is determined by the project.
- The WBS identifies all the work that must be performed to meet project objectives and only those tasks that are truly necessary.

broad overview of the project. It provides enough information to the decision-makers to determine if the project should proceed.

In the Planning process of the project, the decision to proceed has been made and it is time to be more detailed in describing the project. One of the best ways to do this is to use a methodology called the Work Breakdown Structure (WBS), which uses a logical structure to define various levels of detail. It is a tool that is used throughout the project as a building block for other applications. The WBS is one of the most important tools that a project manager has.

The WBS starts at the broadest level and becomes more detailed. The WBS defines the tasks or actions that are necessary to produce a deliverable. Every task or effort detailed in a WBS should be directed towards producing a project deliverable. The project deliverable must always be kept in mind when developing a WBS.

Another key point when writing a WBS is to use a *verb + object* format. For example, *write + parking standards* uses the *verb + object* format. *Write* is the verb and *parking standards* is the object. Using this format will always keep the ultimate deliverable in mind. Let's look at how this might appear in a couple of different formats.

Figure 4-1 shows a WBS in an outline format. You can see that it starts at a very broad level and works down to more specific tasks. Each upper level statement is supported and "built" by the lower level items under it.

An outline format is an excellent first step in writing a WBS. It is simple to organize. No special tools are required other than a word processor. The next step should include putting the WBS in a graphical format.

Figure 4-1. A WBS Using an Outline Format

1.0   Develop a Capital Improvement Plan

    1.1   Collect Data

        1.1.1   Conduct a Citizen and Local Business Survey

        1.1.2   Review Existing Policy-Setting Documents

            1.1.2.1   Review and Summarize the Local Comprehensive Plan

            1.1.2.2   Review and Summarize the Local Government's Budget

        1.1.3   Collect Current Revenue Sources

    1.2   Analyze Data

        1.2.1   Develop Rollup Summaries of Current Expenditures

        1.2.2   Estimate Costs of Approved Projects

        1.2.3   Project Future Revenues

Figure 4-2 shows the same information exhibited in Figure 4-1, but uses a graphical format instead.

It is very important to spend enough time and energy to prepare a thorough and accurate WBS. The WBS is the foundation for project planning and control. If the WBS is not properly developed, problems will crop up in later stages of managing the project. For example, the WBS is used to develop cost estimates and completion dates. If the WBS is incomplete or inaccurate, the cost estimates and completion dates will be meaningless.

The Sticky-Note Method for Developing a WBS

Another simple and inexpensive way to develop a WBS is by using sticky notes. Start by writing the final project deliverable on one sticky note and put it on a wall or window in a room. Continue as you would using a word processor, only use sticky notes. Under each deliverable, write a *verb + object* statement on a sticky note for tasks that must be performed to produce the deliverable. Place the sticky notes in the appropriate location on the wall or window. This can be an excellent team-building exercise for the project team. It will also help everyone on the team understand the key components of the plan.

Figure 4-2. A WBS Using a Graphical Format

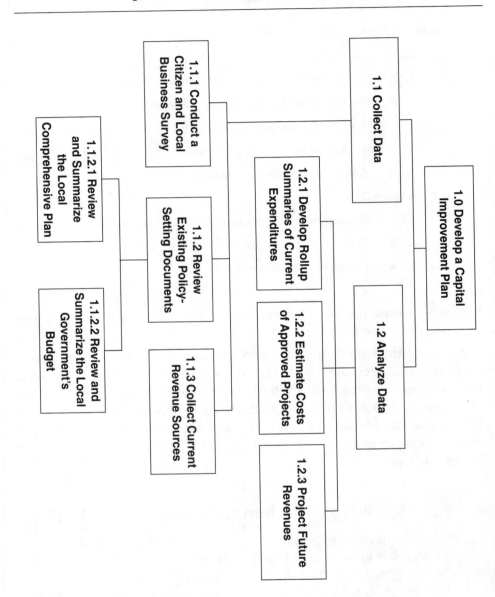

Figure 4-3. Precedence Diagram

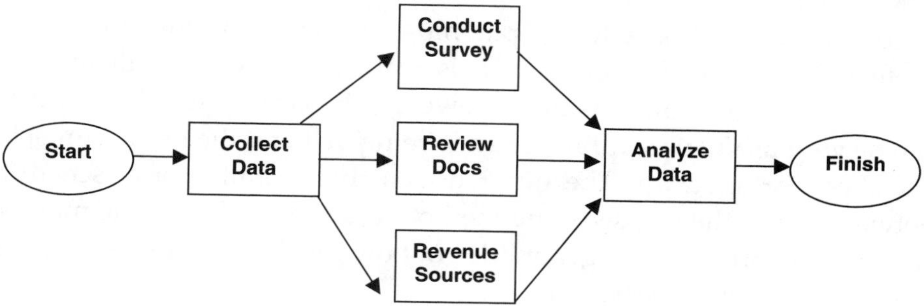

Project Sequencing

Project sequencing involves putting the tasks of the project in a logical series of steps. It is important to remember that, at this point, only logic is being applied and not available resources. This involves taking the WBS and determining which tasks must be performed before other tasks can be started or completed. An individual—or better yet, a group—that is intimately familiar with how the project is prepared must perform this determination of "dependencies."

A detailed WBS must be used to prepare a realistic sequence of the project. The intent is to identify all of the tasks or activities to be performed in order to produce the final product or deliverable.

A precedence diagram is a visual aid that represents the sequence of a project. Figure 4-3 relates to the previous example of preparing a capital improvement plan. For purposes of illustration, the higher level tasks have been used for the diagram.

As shown in Figure 4-3, the three tasks involved with "Collect Data" must occur before the data is analyzed in the next major task. Obviously, there can be many more tasks involved with collecting or analyzing data and these would be represented in the precedence diagram.

Project Schedule

When developing a project schedule, it is important to consider two concepts:

1. *Elapsed Time* (the amount of time it will take to complete a task, regardless of outside considerations such as vacations, sick leave and weekends)

2. *Working Time* (the amount of time that is available to work on the tasks, taking into account time-consumers like vacations, sick leave and weekends)

For purposes of scheduling planning projects, working time is the preferred method of estimation. It is realistic and will result in more projects coming in on schedule. However, the concept of elapsed time can be very useful if deadlines are not being met and the project must be "crashed" or sped up. The difference in the overall project schedule between using the elapsed-time method and the working-time method can give the project manager an idea of how much time can be made up if a project is behind schedule.

The process of project scheduling is supported by numerous computer software applications. The most commonly used application is Microsoft® Project. For most planning projects, Microsoft Project will be more than sufficient to meet the project sequencing needs.

Typically, a start date, a completion date, time to complete the task and any dependencies are required inputs to project scheduling software for each task.

• The *start date* is the specific calendar date that a task will begin. This is especially important for planning projects because this will "anchor" the task to one date on the calendar.

• The *completion date* is the day that the task must be completed. Again, this is represented by a day, month and year.

• *Time to complete* is an estimate in days or hours of the amount of time it will take to complete the task. This is sometimes called "task duration." There are many ways to calculate how much time it will take to complete a task. The best method is to request that the person most familiar with the task estimate the time needed to complete the task based on past experience.

• *Dependencies* must also be considered when scheduling a project. Identifying dependencies will allow the project manager and team to identify which tasks must be prepared in sequence and which tasks may be prepared in parallel or concurrently.

The critical path of a project is an important concept when preparing and analyzing a project schedule. The critical path is the series of tasks from beginning to end of a project or deliverable that has the longest time to complete. In other words, if any task within the critical path is delayed, the final completion date will be delayed. Each task on the critical path must be completed on or before its target date or the project

Table 4-1. Preparing a Planning Project Deliverable for a Public Meeting

Task	Start Date	Completion Date	Duration (Working Time)
Prepare Draft Document	July 2, 2001	July 27, 2001	19 days
Advertise Public Meeting	July 18, 2001	July 18, 2001	1 day
Hold Public Meeting	August 1, 2001	August 1, 2001	1 day
Revise Document	August 2, 2001	August 31, 2001	22 days

will come in late. All modern project scheduling software will calculate the critical path for a project.

Quite often, planning projects are prepared with public input gathered through public meetings. Interim deliverables are drafted, reviewed in a public forum and then revised based upon public input. In addition, the public meetings may need to be noticed or advertised a certain amount of time prior to the public meeting. All of these steps must be put into a project schedule if it is to be accurate and meaningful.

Let's take a look at how that might appear for a project using a table to calculate the schedule. Table 4-1 represents the general components of preparing a draft deliverable for a planning project that must also be reviewed in an advertised public meeting.

The information provided in Table 4-1 can be represented in a number of ways. Precedence diagrams show sequencing and dependencies; they can also include start and completion dates and durations. Gantt charts are another graphical way to represent tasks, dependencies, start and completion dates and durations. Gantt charts are horizontal bar graphs with tasks on the vertical (y) axis and time on the horizontal (x) axis. Figure 4-5 is an example of a simple Gantt chart for the information in Table 4-1. In the chart, the lines represent durations and the **X** ("Hold Public Meeting") represents a project milestone.

Gantt charts can be especially useful to show overlapping tasks and critical dates. Examining overlapping tasks can show when the project team might be overloaded or support staff underutilized. Project milestones, like the public meeting shown in Figure 4-5, are also clearly shown and the tasks that feed those critical dates are itemized.

Figure 4-5. Gantt Chart

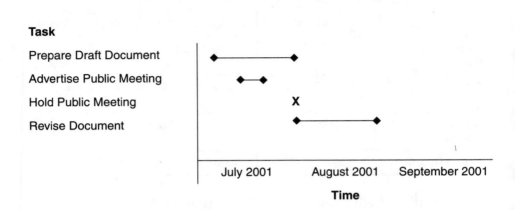

When preparing a project schedule, the bottom line is to be realistic. A project only gets more complicated once it is underway. The most common mistakes made by project managers are not planning for enough time to perform tasks and to coordinate the project. This cannot be over-emphasized. Planners have an advantage in this regard because we regularly estimate how long tasks or other future events will take. We have much more experience with the realities of implementing plans and projects. As a result, we are more aware of the day-to-day issues that arise when trying to make a plan become reality.

Cost Estimating

Estimating the cost of a planning project is a fairly simple and straight-forward effort, although not always easy and accurate. Do not assume that, since the process is simple, the product will necessarily be accurate.

The accuracy of the cost estimate will be determined by the reliability—or robustness—of the WBS. If the WBS has been prepared with an eye towards completeness, the cost estimate will be much more accurate.

The project cost estimation at this Planning stage of the project is much more detailed than the cost estimation done at the Initiating process (described in Chapter 3). At the Initiating process, the costing is used primarily to provide the decision-makers with an estimate of the overall project costs. During the Planning process, a much more specific and reliable project cost estimate is performed. The results of the cost estimation performed during the Planning process of the project will be the cost to which the project manager and team will be held.

Essentially, the cost estimate for a planning project consists of five components:

1. *Time or Labor* (the number of hours that each team member will spend on each project task)

2. *Materials* (supplies that will be needed to complete the project such as paper, office space and meeting supplies)

3. *Equipment* (may include computers, fax machines and vehicles)

4. *Overhead* (associated with personnel such as health insurance, and can also be related to materials or equipment such as heating, air conditioning and electricity)

5. *Outside Vendors* (may include the assistance of planning specialists or attorneys; can also include the use of external print shops for printing draft and final documents)

Job Aid 4-1 offers one way to estimate the costs of a project. As you can see, Job Aid 4-1 relies on the WBS to organize the information. It makes a lot of sense to fall back to the WBS as the framework for the project cost estimate. Using the WBS to organize the cost factors ensures that all of the major costs associated with the project are covered.

Budgeting and Spending

Budgeting and spending issues for a planning project can be complicated. Many planning projects are performed for or by a governmental agency. This can involve a very complicated, bureaucratic and sometimes cumbersome budgeting and cost accounting system. As a result, the budgeting and spending plan for a planning project must take into account the context of the "client's" system.

Questions to consider when addressing the budgeting and spending aspects of a project include the following:

• *What are the procurement requirements and processes involved in purchasing goods and services?* If the client and project team work for the same organization, the answer to this question will be much easier than if the client and project team are from different organizations. If, for example, a consultant is the project manager for the development of a comprehensive plan for a county, the consultant will need to understand how the county's procurement process operates. This will be important for invoicing, payments, advertising and notification requirements for buying outside materials or services that will be required to complete the project on time.

- *What are the reporting requirements for the client?* If the client is a public agency, they will need to regularly report to the city council or county commission on the status of their expenditures for the project. Knowing when and in what form those reports must be prepared can greatly influence how the project team summarizes the status of the project.

- *How are budget adjustments or corrections made?* If the client has an established process for revising and updating the project's budget, this should be known and documented by the project manager during the Planning process of the project. If it takes three to six months to revise and get final approval for any project budget items, the project manager needs to understand and plan for this.

- *What internal and external budgetary reviews will be needed for the project?* Depending on the size and influence of the planning project, the budget may need to be reviewed by internal departments or committees as well as external citizen groups and neighborhood or non-profit agencies. They in turn may require their own reporting formats and timelines that could greatly influence the cost and schedule for the project.

- *How are contingency funds handled?* No project budget is exact. A project budget is estimated with as much accuracy as possible; however, the budgeted items may cost more than expected. Because of this reality, it is a common practice to set aside a contingency fund to pay for items that cost more than estimated. It is critical for the project manager to know up front how the client deals with contingency funds, especially if the client is a public agency.

The answers to these questions—and any others that may influence the budgeting process for a project—must be asked, answered and documented during the project's Planning process. This is the time to deal with these issues, not when the project is up and running. The last thing a project manager and client want to have happen is to find out that the project will need to be delayed for three months due to a budgeting issue that, if known early on, could have been avoided.

Communications

A complete and well-thought-out communications component of a project plan is extremely important, particularly for a planning project. There are two major elements of a communications plan.

Internal Communication. The internal communication component involves distributing pertinent information to the project team. The information must be accurate, timely and directed to the right person. These three factors will determine the mode of the communication.

Internal communication can take place in many different forms. The content, timeliness and the recipients should dictate the form. Some of the types of information distribution methods include:

- telephone
- e-mail
- internal memos
- postal service ("snail mail")
- fax
- video conference
- verbal (face to face)

Each form of communication listed above has its strengths and weaknesses. For example, verbal communication can take place quickly and effectively by two people crossing paths in the hallway if they work in the same building. However, requiring a widely dispersed project team to come together for a team meeting can be timely and very expensive, and therefore should be used sparingly.

External Communication. As with internal communication, the content, timeliness and audience greatly influence the form of external information distribution activities. External communication can be an especially important and critical piece for a planning project. Involving external parties and the press can make or break a planning project. Great care must be taken when developing the external communication method for a planning project.

Types of external communication forms include:

- public meetings
- press releases
- interviews with the press and editorial boards
- handouts and publications
- visual aids
- radio and television announcements
- Internet site

The message, time factor and audience must all be considered when determining the most appropriate form of external communication. Regardless of the form of communication, accuracy and consistency of the message is vital to the success of a planning project.

For a planning project to be successful, it must be well received by the public, elected officials, decision-makers and special interest groups. For a project to be well received, it must be explained accurately and repeatedly to the affected and interested parties. The importance of the communication component of a project plan cannot be overemphasized.

Project Risks

Project risks are any internal or external action that may affect the schedule, cost or scope of a project. The purpose of addressing project risk is to determine what potential risks exist, how they might affect a project and identify what actions can be taken by a project manager if or when they occur.

Planners have a leg up on other professionals when dealing with project risk during the Planning process of a project. As planners, we make a living from anticipating the future. Project risk planning is simply an organized way to assess what might happen in the middle of a project and then establish how to respond before it happens.

There are three components of project risk planning: (1) risk identification; (2) risk analysis; and (3) risk response. Numerous books have been written on project risk planning. This book provides a brief overview of the subject; the reader can consult the other resources to investigate the topic in depth.

Risk Identification. The easiest and most cost-effective method of identifying potential risks to a project is to consult with experienced project managers and planners familiar with the particular project being undertaken. For example, if the project is to develop a new sign ordinance for a municipality, the project manager can consult with other planners who have written or managed the development of a sign ordinance. During discussions, the project manager for the new project should ask questions such as:

- How long did it take you to develop the sign ordinance?
- What kind of unanticipated factors influenced the schedule for the ordinance?
- How did you handle input from citizens and affected parties?
- If you were to start over, what would you do differently?
- What would you do the same?
- What are the threats to developing a new sign ordinance?

Job Aid 4-2 offers a generic questionnaire that can be used to identify the potential risks of a project. These kinds of interviews can be done

Figure 4-6. Risk Components

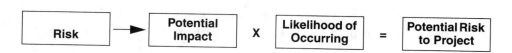

Table 4-2. Qualitative Risk Analysis

Risk	Potential Impact	Likelihood of Occurring	Potential Risk to Project
Insufficient Funds	High	Medium	Medium
Insufficient Staff	Medium	High	High
Not Accepted by Chamber of Commerce	High	Low	Medium

individually or in group brainstorming formats. Flow charts and diagrams can be used to represent the various threats identified. It is important to mention that a risk is any event that can have a positive or negative impact on a project. A positive event is considered a risk if it has the potential of changing the project's scope, schedule or cost.

Risk Analysis. Risk analysis basically does two things: (1) determines the potential impact of a risk; and (2) estimates the potential for the risk to occur. Analyzing these two factors will help the project manager prioritize the risks. This will allow the project manager to identify those risks that have the greatest potential to affect the project. Figure 4-6 portrays how the components of risk relate to each other.

Risks to projects can be analyzed qualitatively or quantitatively. Table 4-2 shows how the risks associated with a new sign ordinance can be analyzed qualitatively.

Recognizing that Table 4-2 represents a simplified example, it is easy to see how the project manager and team can quickly identify the potential high risks to a project. Job Aid 4-3 provides a chart for assessing qualitative project risk. For most planning projects, a qualitative risk analysis will suffice. However, on extremely complex and expensive projects, a quantitative risk analysis may be appropriate. It is beyond the scope of this book to address quantitative risk analyses. Several books on project risk are listed in the Resources section of this chapter.

Risk Response. A series of responses must be identified and written down for each project risk. If the time is taken during the Planning process to document the actions to be taken in the event of a risk, the potential for the project to be a success increases dramatically. Think of how much time is wasted and useless energy is spent when responding to a risk or emergency when people don't know what to do. A kind of panic can even set in. It is the same for project risks.

The response to a project risk must take into account the type and severity of the risk. Information pertaining to risk identification and risk analysis (as described earlier) is critical to determining the appropriate course of response action. The response, time frame and person responsible for the response must be documented and distributed to the project team before the project begins.

Using Outside Vendors or Consultants

When developing a project plan, it is important to consider the use of external vendors or consultants. Due to the nature of planning projects, it is unusual for the project manager to require vendors for materials or goods. For most planning projects, the consideration is whether to use consultants to help with the technical and legal aspects of the project.

When considering using external consultants for a planning project, the project manager will be concerned about the following three factors:

1.   *People.* Are there enough people assigned or available to work on the project? This is a question of quantity of staff to get the work done. Of course, their talent, knowledge and experience will influence the number of staff. There is still a basic minimum number of workers needed to get the work done. If there is not enough staff to get the work done, the project manager should consider hiring an outside consultant or group to work on the project.

2.   *Time.* What are the overall time constraints of the project? If there is enough time to allow staff to work individually on the project, or if there are gaps in the schedule that give the project manager options on moving staff around to work on various tasks over time, there may not be a need to hire outside workers. However, if the project is under tight time constraints, or if the project manager identifies specific times when additional people will be needed to get through a crunch time, he/she should weigh the possibility of hiring an outside person or group of people to work on the project.

3. ***Content.*** Sometimes a project team has enough people and time to complete a project on time and within budget, but lacks a specific talent or expertise on the team. For example, a planning project may require the services of an experienced statistician to interpret the results of a citizen survey on a project. The project manager should anticipate these needs and plan on bringing in the talent when it is needed.

The Project Plan

Once all of the components of the Planning process are complete, the project plan must be prepared. The size and format of the plan will be determined by the project itself. The important point to remember is that the project planning information should be put into one document.

After the project plan has been completed, the project team, the project sponsor and the client or customer must review it. For planning projects, this will usually include a review by the public in the form of special interest groups, planning advisory committees or elected officials.

One of the most important responsibilities of a project manager—especially a project manager of a planning project—is getting approval of the project plan by the sponsor, affected parties and the client. The absolute worst thing that can happen to a project manager is to spend months or even years working on a planning project only to find that, when it is completed, it is not what the public or the client had in mind. This horrendous mistake can only be avoided by taking the time to prepare a thorough project plan, and to ensure that it meets the needs and expectations of the affected and elected parties—and the final customer.

REVIEW

- Planners are ideally suited to prepare the second process of a project (the project plan).
- To be successful, a project manager must pay particular attention to the Planning process.
- The project description using a WBS is the foundation of any project.
- Project sequencing and scheduling deal with the logic and time constraints of project tasks.
- The costs for each task must be estimated to arrive at an overall project cost.
- The project manager must identify in the project plan how expenditures and budgeting will be addressed during the project.

- One of the most important parts of a project plan for a planning project is the communications component involving internal and external forms of communication.
- Identifying the potential risks of a project early on can make or break a project.
- The use of outside vendors and consultants is another piece of the puzzle for a project plan that can make the difference between a successful planning project and one that is a failure.
- The project plan should include all of the components identified above, and any other deemed appropriate by the project manager, and must receive approval by affected parties, the client and customers.

Job Aid 4-1. Project Cost Estimation

Task from WBS	Labor Cost Estimate (hours multiplied by wages)	Materials	Equipment	Overhead	Subtotal
Total					

Job Aid 4-2. Project Risk Questionnaire

Project Name: _____   Date: _____

Person Interviewed: _____

1. How long did the project take to complete?
2. What unanticipated factors influenced the project schedule?
3. How did you handle public input?
4. If you were to start the project over, what would you do differently?
5. What would you do the same?
6. What were the threats to completing the project on time and within budget?

Job Aid 4-3. Qualitative Project Risk Assessment

Risk	Potential Impact (High/Medium /Low)	Likelihood of Occurring (High/Medium /Low)	Potential Risk to Project (High/Medium /Low)

RESOURCES

Chapman, Chris, and Stephen Ward. *Project Risk Management, Processes, Techniques and Insights.* New York, NY: John Wiley and Sons, 1997.

Grey, Stephen. *Practical Risk Assessment for Project Management.* New York, NY: John Wiley and Sons, 1998.

Kanabar, Vijay. *Project Risk Management.* Acton, MA: Copley Custom Publication Group, 1997.

Raferty, J. *Risk Analysis in Project Management.* New York, NY: Chapman & Hall, 1994.

Termini, Michael J. *Strategic Project Management: Tools and Techniques for Planning, Decision Making, and Implementation.* Dearborn, MI: Society of Manufacturing Engineers, 1999.

5

Executing

Don't bother about genius. Don't worry about being clever. Trust to hard work, perseverance and determination.

—Sir Frederick Treves

Want to release your potential? Help others release theirs.

—Pat Lynch

There are some people who live in a dream world, and there are some who face reality; and then there are those who turn one into the other.

—Douglas Everett

INTERVIEW

Sonny Princeton is a 64-year-old planning commissioner for a small town in New England. Sonny has been on the town planning commission for 12 years. She also has over 27 years of planning experience as a practicing planner, including a stint as a planning director. Ms. Princeton has been an adjunct professor at the local community college for the last seven years where she teaches an introduction to planning course. *PMfP* interviewed Sonny to get her thoughts on the third process of project management: Executing.

PMfP: Sonny, you have a lot of practical, hands-on planning experience at many different levels. Should project management be important to planners?

Sonny: Absolutely! I see it all the time. A well-intentioned planner tackles a worthwhile project and applies all of the latest planning techniques he or she learned in school. The project is well thought out, supported by the community and even starts off on the right foot. Everything seems to be moving along fine.

PMfP: Then what happens?

Sonny: Nothing! Money is spent, people are utilized and time passes by, but there is nothing to show for it. The project never gets done. The community begins to ask questions and, before you know it, the planner is looking for a new job.

PMfP: What is the problem?

Sonny: The planner may know a lot about planning, but he or she knows very little about managing a project. They know the latest GIS techniques but don't know a thing about how to get others to work together towards a common goal or deliverable. It's a real shame.

PMfP: How can this be avoided?

Sonny: Executing the project plan requires a different set of skills, abilities and knowledge—competencies, if you will—than the average planner has coming right out of college. Even experienced planners could use some of the discipline and strategies offered by the project management approach.

PMfP: Give us some specifics.

Sonny: For one thing, basic management strategies can be implemented such as ensuring that the financial and staffing resources have actually been committed to the project as originally promised. Second—and what I consider to be the most important factor—is applying people skills in order to build a team that is focused on getting the job done. Now, I know it is a lot easier said than done, but if we as planners are going to be successful, we need to expand our professionals skills toolbox.

PMfP: You seem to know a lot about project management.

Sonny: I have seen many good planners start out well and then flounder in the execution of a project. As planners, we have done a lot of good, but we can do so much more with additional skills under our belt.

PMfP: Thanks for your time.

Sonny: Thanks for having me.

EXECUTING

Project execution is the third process of project management. It is estimated that project execution should take approximately 25% of a project manager's time (see Table 3-1 in Chapter 3). In other words, 75% of the project manager's time should be spent on the other four processes of project management.

A common misconception is that all, or most, of the project manager's time and effort should be spent on executing—or "doing"—the project. If a project manager is managing his/her time and project team well, most of their time will be spent on other processes of the project life cycle.

What does executing a project mean? Essentially, this is when the project manager turns on his/her people skills. In this process, the project manager leads the team through the tasks and assignments of the project by applying communication skills, monitoring the team's progress, managing conflicts and change, conducting meetings and motivating the team members.

Project execution is when the project plan becomes real and tangible through implementation by the people on the team. Remember: the project is the result of work by people, and the primary responsibility of a project manager is to work with people to ensure that the project plan is implemented. This seems like such a simple and basic fact; however, many project managers forget that their main function is to work with other people to get the project completed.

Planners have an enormous advantage over many other professionals in this arena of people skills and leadership. As planners, we are trained and experienced in dealing with people. Our entire professional emphasis is on creating places that are supported, used and influenced by people. In fact, we are energized by the fact that the main reason we chose this profession is that we want to make our physical environment a better place for human beings.

It makes sense that we will have a leg up on other professions when it comes to being project managers in general and with the Executing process specifically.

Committing Project Resources

In earlier sections of the book, we spoke about the importance of identifying the best people and the necessary resources available to work on the project. Senior managers and line managers were contacted in preparation of the Project Charter. They were asked for staff from their organizational units who will be asked to work on the team. Estimates were made of how much of the team member's time was needed on the project.

It is important to remember that, in most organizations, the line managers (not the project managers) have control over who and when staff will work on the project. Negotiating with the line managers to get "their" staff to work on the project is an extremely important responsibility of the project manager. This is when friendships, past mistakes and shared histories will come into play.

The project manager must get a commitment by the line manager to use their staff on the project. The degree of formality of the commitment will vary depending on the complexity of the project and the policies and procedures of the organization. However, the commitment, when received, should be put into writing to confirm the following:

- Who is going to work on the project?
- When they will work on the project?
- How much of their time will be required?
- To whom will they report when working on the project?

The project manager must make certain that the line manager and/or supervisor of the person being requested to work on the project acknowledges in some way receipt and understanding of the above information. The form of this agreement may be a formal memo, a procedural process through the human resources department (like a temporary reassignment), or an e-mail between the project manager and line manager. The important thing to remember is to get it in writing and to get the line manager's approval. Job Aid 5-1 is an example of an agreement for staff assignment from a line manager to a project team.

If physical resources or equipment are required on the project, the project manager must now begin the process of procuring the resources. Procurement processes vary a great deal among different organizations. The project manager must become familiar with the process in his/her organization to ensure that the procurement process does not delay the execution of the project.

Implementing the Project Plan

"Implementing the project" simply means getting the project team to put into action the tasks of the project plan. It is time to begin "working on the work." The most effective way to begin implementing the project plan is to have a project team kickoff meeting.

The project kickoff meeting is the formal start of the project for the project team. This is when the project manager puts his/her facilitation and motivation skills to practice. The kickoff meeting should have all of the key project team members present. On small- to medium-sized projects, this will mean the entire project team. It may not be practical or desirable to have all of the team members on very large projects get together at the same time in the same place. However, on most planning projects, the entire team should be present at the kickoff meeting.

At a minimum, the agenda for the project team kickoff meeting should include:

- communicating the goals and objectives of the project
- introducing the team members to each other and explaining their respective roles on the project
- clearly identifying the final project deliverables
- explaining the project timeline and major milestones
- identifying key customers and stakeholders of the project
- clearly stating that the project has now begun
- describing the plan for communicating with project team members

Job Aid 5-2 presents a sample agenda for the project kickoff meeting. It is important for the project manager to model the type of behavior that he/she wants the team members to follow. The meeting should start on time and be professionally facilitated. The project culture or environment begins with the project team kickoff meeting. The project manager should also pass out important information in writing to the team members at the meeting. The written materials should be well designed and bound, if possible.

Managing Project Progress

Managing project progress is different than controlling the project, which is the next chapter in this book. Managing the progress of the project deals with the day-to-day people management and leadership by the project manager.

This would be a good time to clarify the difference between a planner who is managing a project and a project manager with a planning background. A planner managing a project is characterized by the following traits:

- always gets into the technical planning details of the project
- rarely lets project team members do the work they were hired to do
- feels as though "the best way to get the work done is to do it yourself," and then does it
- forgets that other professionals can also be good at what they do

- figures that, since you are the planner running the project, you should do all of the talking at public and team meetings
- becomes irritated because nobody else seems to be doing his/her job

Sound familiar? These traits are not uncommon and are not limited to the planning profession, although I do think it is sometimes more difficult for planners to step back and manage a planning project than other professionals simply because we enjoy our technical work so much. However, if a planner is going to be a successful project manager, he/she must temporarily remove their planning cloak and put on the project manager cloak.

This doesn't mean that the manager of planning projects doesn't need to be familiar with planning. It does mean, however, that a good project manager lets their team members do what they are good at. At times, the project manager may have to remove his/her project manager's hat and put on a planner's hat to prepare or review technical planning documents. However, the primary responsibility of a project manager is to manage the project—not do all of the technical work.

Therefore, a project manager with a planning background has the following characteristics:

- keeps the big picture and final project deliverables in mind
- lets the team members do most of the technical work
- manages the process more than individual tasks
- spends most of their time on people issues like communication, problem solving and performance
- makes sure the necessary resources are available for team members to do their work
- leads the team through goal clarification, team building and motivation

Management and Personality Styles

As you can see, a good project manager has a solid set of people management skills. The project manager must work through other people to get the work done. This is a good time to briefly address management and personality styles. You may be wondering, "Why is it important to discuss management and personality styles in a book about project management for planners?" A good project manager should be familiar with management and personality styles for the following reasons:

Figure 5-1. Theory X and Theory Y

Tough Judgmental Parent		Benevolent Patriarch Nurturing Parent

Theory X—Parent/Child

External Control		Self-control

Theory Y—Adult/Adult

- *To be able to deal with the assumption that "my world is the real world."* Not everyone views the world as we do and that fact affects human relationships.

- *To be able to "flex" or adapt to another's style.* In order to communicate effectively with others, it is sometimes beneficial to speak in their language or style.

- *To be able to perform meaningful team-building sessions.* Good teams are made up of a wide variety of management and personality styles. The diversity of styles is a strength in good teams when managed properly.

Theory X and Theory Y. Douglas McGregor, in his classic book on management entitled *The Human Side of Enterprise*, describes the Theory X and Theory Y management styles. Figure 5-1 presents these two styles in a graph.

Theory X management style is all about external control. A Theory X manager views his/her subordinates as children and interacts with them as such. They assume that their view is the correct view and that the subordinate's view is invalid or meaningless. In the eyes of a Theory X manager, "I'm okay, you're not okay" is the dominant attitude. As such, Theory X managers can range from being judgmental to nurturing, depending on their perception of the "child" or subordinate.

Theory Y managers, on the other hand, view individuals as having the potential for self-control and treat them that way. A Theory Y manager believes that the individual is intrinsically motivated to do a good job; all they need are the proper knowledge, skills and resources. A Theory Y manager views the world as "I'm okay, you're okay." To Theory Y managers, subordinates are adults too, and should be treated that way.

Entire books have been written about the Theory X and Theory Y styles of management. We don't have time to cover the topic in great detail here. However, the take-home message is that a good project manager should know their own style and that of their teams, and use this knowledge to manage to the benefit of both. Job Aid 5-3 provides a more detailed description of the Theory X and Theory Y management styles.

Personality Styles. Based on the work of Carl Jung, four personality styles have been identified that provide insight into the way people view and interact with the world. These four styles have been used to develop a number of different personality assessment tools—the most common being the Myers-Briggs personality type indicator.

The four personality styles recognized by Jung are:

1. *Intuitive.* The Intuitive person is future-focused and prefers to deal with concepts and possibilities. They are creative, "right-brained," dominant people that prefer open-ended, nonlinear thinking. Intuitive people do not need closure and can work in a wide open environment.

2. *Thinker.* Thinkers are analytical people who prefer closure to issues and problems. They are concerned with correctness and think in a linear, past-present-future reference. Thinkers love to analyze issues as long as a conclusion is reached and the loop closed. They are considered "left-brained" thinkers.

3. *Feeler.* Feelers have very developed emotional antennae. They are concerned with the harmonious effect of decisions. Feelers prefer to deal with the past and have strong ties to people. They are most interested in the impacts that decisions have on others.

4. *Sensor.* Sensors prefer action and expediency in decision-making processes. A Sensor "doesn't want it right, they want it now." They enjoy and are capable of juggling many tasks at the same time.

Jung and others readily admit that we all have some characteristics from each of the four styles and that we are a combination of each. However, people usually have a dominant style that characterizes their overall interactions with other people and the world. Knowing that personality styles exist among their team members can help project managers choose a style of communication and motivation that is most effective.

Project Team Meetings

Earlier in this chapter, we spoke about the project team kickoff meeting and how that should be organized. Once the project is up and running, it is important for the project manager to periodically hold project team meetings. The following guidelines should be considered when deciding when to hold team meetings.

Topics. The primary purpose of team meetings is to provide team members with a status report on the project and to identify any problems or constraints. Therefore, task managers should provide short briefings on important topics. The other main topic for the meetings should be identification of any problems or constraints that have arisen. The team should discuss the problems and determine the best course of action. In addition, let us not forget about the importance of team building as a function of a meeting. Team-building exercises should be built into every project team meeting to help the team break down organizational and communication barriers so that they can work better together.

Duration. The key word when discussing team meeting duration is "brief." These do not have to be marathon sessions; in fact, they should *not* be marathon sessions. All of the team members are busy working on this project and probably a few others. Respect their time and schedules by ensuring that the meeting progresses at a good pace. The planner as a project manager has a leg up on other professionals when it comes to facilitating meetings and should use those skills in running the meeting.

Frequency. The frequency of team meetings should be determined by the specifics of the project. If a lot is happening of which the team members need to be aware, meetings might be held as frequently as twice a month. At other times, team meetings may only need to occur every two to three months, depending on the status and issues of the project. The project manager must use his/her judgment when determining whether or not to hold a team meeting. A team meeting where all of the key players get together in one room should be held only if no other form of communication can deal with the issues to be discussed. Due to time, money and travel constraints, a meeting should be the last resort.

Tone. The tone, or atmosphere, of the meetings should be fun and informative. It's okay to have fun at meetings and laugh a little. They don't need to be serious, somber affairs. The project manager should not embarrass team members by holding silly events; however, working a little levity and humor into the meetings will make the team members interact more productively and be less resistant to future meetings.

Fire Fighting

Fighting fires is part of a project manager's job profile. How a project manager deals with unexpected and unwanted issues as they come up can be a determining factor between a successful project manager and one that is unsuccessful.

As part of the project plan, we discussed risk management. The project plan should include predetermined strategies on how to handle anticipated issues when they arise. When those issues come up, the project manager should follow the protocol identified in the risk management portion of the project plan.

In this section, we are talking about the unknowns: the problems that arise that we had no possibility of identifying as part of the risk management plan. This is when the project manager must respond in a professional manner, consistent with the objectives of the project and the values of the team and operating organization.

The issue of fighting fires is mentioned here because it is a reality, and the project manager must be prepared to deal with them when they arise and not hope that "If I ignore the problem, it will go away." Problems never go away when they are ignored; they only get worse. The risk management plan may have a generic protocol for responding to unplanned events; however, due to the nature of "fires," the project manager will need to deal with them in an appropriate fashion when they arise on a case-by-case basis.

Communicating Project Progress

Project team members and stakeholders must be kept apprised of the status of the project. In the previous chapter of this book, we spoke about developing a communications plan for the project, which is implemented during the Executing process. This is when the various communication strategies are taken, and appropriate people and organizations kept up to speed through the project.

It is important to emphasize how important communication is to the success of planning projects. Planning projects, by their very nature, are social projects. They impact people. As such, the people working on the planning project and those impacted by it all have a vested interest in its progress and outcome. Therefore, how and when the status of the project is communicated to team members and affected parties is critical to any project's success, especially for planning projects.

Depending on the size and complexity of the project, the project manager may or may not be the person in charge of carrying out the communication strategies. The method in which the plan's progress is communicated may be the responsibility of several team members. The project manager is responsible for ensuring that an effective communications strategy is developed and implemented.

Following are some important considerations when executing a communications plan to team members and interested parties:

Honesty. At all costs and at all times, the information disseminated to the team members and affected public must be accurate and true. This seems like such a simple and basic fact; however, when the plan is underway and deadlines are looming, the truth can get lost in the message. If a planning project and its manager are going to have credibility with the people on the team and the people affected by it, the information they provide must be accurate. It is the project manager's job to ensure that the message is factual, or the messenger and planning project will be doomed.

Consistency. It is also very important for the recipients of the messages to receive consistent information. They should not hear different "truths" from different people on the status of the project. All messengers must be singing from the same song sheet. The project manager must distribute the same information to all people and not be selective depending on the audience.

Timeliness. The right information must get to the right people at the right time. It does no good if accurate and thorough project status reports are distributed so late that they are meaningless. The project manager must stay vigilant in distributing information to team members and the public.

Format. Different audiences demand different types of information and in differing forms. For example, a traffic engineer on a planning project will require very detailed information from the project manager on the status of population projections, and it will need to be in a specific format for it to be of any use. On the other hand, a citizen on an advisory board may only need to know a general rollup of the projections and the methodologies used in arriving at them. It is the same information, only formatted differently to reflect the needs of the audience.

Implementing Quality Assurance Procedures

Project managers need to be concerned with three components of a project: time, resources and quality (or scope). For many projects, the matter of quality is quantifiable and measurable. For example, a construction project must be built according to industry specifications. Concrete must meet certain hardness requirements, and buildings must be constructed according to very detailed design and architectural drawings. In the case of information technology projects, software must meet an acceptable error standard. Manufacturing projects must be able to produce within a predetermined failure rate.

Planning projects are a little different. In many cases, the quality of a planning project is determined by how well it is accepted by a community of citizens. Does a comprehensive plan meet the expectations of the surrounding residents? Is the architectural design of a new shopping center consistent with the adjacent buildings and local neighborhood? Does a wetlands protection ordinance go far enough to appease the environmental community, but not too far to alienate the development community?

These are all very difficult questions to answer regarding the quality of a planning project. If planners can be faulted in this area at all, we can be criticized for being perfectionists. We want our planning projects to be *perfect!* We often feel that, if a plan isn't perfect, it shouldn't see the light of day. This is a professional character defect that must be controlled through well-thought-out quality assurance procedures. As planners, we must put our desire to have the perfect project on the back burner to ensure that we are able to meet timelines and budgets. Perfection is a fine goal; however, we must be willing to accept something less in order to complete a project on time without blowing the budget.

Ultimately, the question comes down to "How good is good enough?" When can we, as project managers, sign off on the quality of a deliverable, confident that it meets acceptable professional and community quality standards and expectations?

For each major planning project deliverable, a series of questions must be answered:

Is it safe? At a minimum, all safety codes and ordinances must be followed. For example, cul-de-sacs must be designed and built to meet the requirements of emergency vehicle access, and pedestrian walkways must allow people to walk within a well-protected pathway.

Is it consistent with the local community standards and expectations? This is a difficult question to answer for planning projects. At a minimum, the local citizens should review the plan. They must be given an opportunity to comment on its goals and design. Participation can go a long way to appease citizen concerns regarding the planning project.

Does it meet professional planning standards? As planners, we have an obligation to ensure that the methodologies used in developing a plan are consistent with acceptable planning principles. Have we followed the proper quantitative methods in surveys? Have we compromised our professional ethics during the project?

As stated earlier, quality assurance is not an easy task for managers of planning projects. However, the fact that quality assurance may be difficult does not mean that we should put blinders on and fail to consider it when executing a project. We must make sure that the plan meets acceptable standards and expectations, *and* that it does not suffer from being held to unrealistic and unachievable perfectionist criteria.

Leading the Team

A project manager is the leader of the project team. It is as simple as that. He/she is responsible for the team's:

- direction
- time management
- resources
- morale
- communication
- protection from outside influences

It is the project manager's job to make sure that the project team is cohesive and not just a group of individuals. This is a daunting and time-consuming aspect of being a project manager.

Typically, setting aside the necessary time to manage and lead the project team is given very little consideration by most project managers. Team leadership is an area that planners have a leg up on most other professionals. We are accustomed to pulling together a widely diverse group of individuals and getting them to agree on common goals. We realize that the heart of a project—or community—is really a collection of people. Planners also appreciate that people need to work together towards a common goal.

There are a lot of books, videos and training exercises on the subject of leadership. The same competencies that make up a good leader in an organization are important to a project manager. Some of these resources are listed at the end of this chapter and in Chapter 9.

Leadership is something that can be learned and developed by individuals. It requires self-awareness, knowledge and the discipline to carry it out. It is not something that is developed without effort. Becoming a good leader generally takes time, hard work and desire, combined with a willingness and ability to take risks. Successful projects have good leaders.

REVIEW

- Executing the project is the third process of project management and should only comprise approximately 25% of the project manager's time on the overall project.
- Project execution is when the project plan is implemented.
- Planners have a leg up on most other professionals when it comes to project execution because we have the people skills necessary to perform this function.
- Project resources must be committed during this process.
- Implementing the plan means action and lots of it.
- The project team kickoff meeting is one of the most important steps in executing the project.
- During the Executing process, a successful project manager must take off their "technical hat" and put on their "manager's hat."
- Periodic meetings and regular communication must take place in order to adequately deal with the "fires" that occasionally arise and to communicate the status of the plan.
- The quality of the deliverables is the responsibility of the project manager.
- A good project manager is also a good leader of people.

Job Aid 5-1. Staff Assignment Agreement

Project Name:
Name of Staff Member Being Assigned:
Calendar Dates of Assignment:
Number of Hours or Percent of Time Assigned to Project:
Short Description of Project Assignment:
_____   _____ Signature of Line Supervisor/Manager   Date
_____   _____ Signature of Project Manager   Date

Job Aid 5-2. Sample Project Team Kickoff Meeting Agenda

Agenda
Project Team Kickoff Meeting
Date, Time, Place

I.   Welcome

II.   Introduction of Team Members

III.   Project Goals and Objectives

IV.   Final Project Deliverables

V.   Project Timeline and Major Milestones

VI.   Key Project Customers and Stakeholders

VII.   Project Work Authorization

VIII.   Plan for Team Communication

IX.   Questions and Answers

X.   Adjourn

Job Aid 5-3. Theory X and Theory Y Management Styles

Manager's Characteristic	Theory X Parent/Child Relationship	Theory Y Adult/Adult Relationship
Manager's View of Work	Work is a source of dissatisfaction. We must compensate for this through pay and benefits.	Work can be satisfying and challenging—a major opportunity to test one's talents and develop them more fully.
Manager's View of Workers	Employees want less responsibility and security. They are dependent on supervisors to make decisions, solve problems, set goals and keep them productive.	Employees want more responsibility and challenge. They are capable of making decisions, solving problems and setting goals for themselves, if we let them.
Manager's View of Self	"I'm okay, you're not okay." People are too dependent on me. I end up having to do their thinking for them and bail them out.	"I'm okay, you're okay." Once they've been trained, my role is that of a coach. I must step back and let them play the game.
Motivation Used by Manager	Carrot and stick: set up system of rewards and punishments to entice and coerce employees.	Work is inherently appealing; use it to give challenge, sense of achievement, recognition, responsibility and growth.
Expectations: the "Pygmalion Effect"	This manager expects less of people than they are capable of—and gets it! "Expect the worst and you won't be surprised."	This manager expects more of people than they knew they were capable of—and gets it! "Expect the best (not perfection) and people will give their best effort."
The Working Relationship	"Employees are here to extend my effectiveness."	"I am here to extend the effectiveness of my employees."
Motivation of Employees	They spend most of their energy keeping the boss happy, harvesting the carrots and avoiding the stick.	They invest their time meeting goals and standards upon which they and the manager have jointly agreed.
The Goal of the Organization for Employees	To have workers trained as well-oiled machines that make few errors, require little maintenance and function as highly dependable robots within a narrowly prescribed area of operations.	To develop people to the point where each is a manager of his/her own time and talent, solving problems and making decisions within an expanding area of freedom and responsibility.

Table adapted from Training House management training materials (2000).

RESOURCES

Jung, Carl. *Psychological Types*. London: Kegan Paul, 1946.

Knowles, Malcolm S., Elwood F. Holton III and Richard A. Swanson. *The Adult Learner: The Definitive Classic in Adult Education and Human Resource Development, 5th Ed.* Houston, TX: Gulf Publishing, 1998.

McGregor, Douglas. *The Human Side of Enterprise*. New York, NY: McGraw-Hill, 1960.

Parker, Glenn M. *Cross-Functional Teams: Working with Allies, Enemies & Other Strangers*. San Francisco, CA: Jossey-Bass, Inc., 1994.

Training House. Management Assessment of Proficiency. Princeton, NJ: Training House, 2000. Web site: http://www.traininghouse.com

6

Controlling

Even if you are on the right track—you'll get run over if you just sit there.

—ARTHUR GODFREY

Not everything that can be counted counts, and not everything that counts can be counted.

—ALBERT EINSTEIN

I have enough money to last me the rest of my life ... unless I buy something.

—JACKIE MASON

INTERVIEW

The subject for this interview is Cliff Demptster. Cliff has six years of local government planning experience and recently started his own planning consulting firm. He is the company. It is a one-man show with his wife helping out with correspondence and the financial books.

PMfP: The subject of this interview is controlling a project. Before we get into that, I have to ask you a question: Wasn't it a bit risky starting your own consulting company with only six years' experience?

Cliff: Yes, I guess so, but everything is risky. It's just a question of how much risk you feel comfortable with. I feel less risk with my own consulting firm because I have complete control over my success or failure.

PMfP: Good point. I guess it does relate to our topic of the Controlling process of project management after all. Tell us what you think of the role of project control.

Cliff: In my mind, proper control of a project is the most important process. For example, I started my own consulting firm. I looked at it as a project. I created a charter, wrote a business plan and started implementing the business plan when I retained my first client. It was after I started "working on the work" that I realized I needed to monitor my cash flow and time management.

PMfP: Tell us more.

Cliff: Well, my first client was my previous employer, Capital City. They wanted me to draft a Parks and Recreation Element for their comprehensive plan. I knew the area, the issues and the data. It made a lot of sense for me to take on this project but, as I started working on the project, I soon realized that drafting a good element was not my only objective if I were to stay in business. I had other objectives that I needed to stay on top of.

PMfP: So having a successful business involves more than just producing good work?

Cliff: Exactly. I needed to manage my time so I could pursue other clients. This job wasn't going to last forever and I had to make sure I had income after I completed the job for the city. Managing my time properly meant that I had to track it and make sure I was spending the right amount of time on the right tasks. So I started a simple timesheet system to monitor the time I spent each day. This way, at the end of the day or the week, I could review how I spent my time and make adjustments to make sure my overall objectives were met.

PMfP: I imagine, as a small firm, you have to be concerned with cash flow as well.

Cliff: You might say that. I don't have any big investors, which means I need to monitor the money coming in and the money going out very closely. Otherwise, I would be out of business before my business cards were printed. This is where my wife Jasmine comes in. She's the financial wizard and the only reason I have stayed in the black so far. Jasmine has started a financial management system that keeps track of every dollar associated with the firm. Without that, I don't know what I would do.

PMfP: You would probably end up trying to get your old job back with the city.

Cliff: Exactly. Jasmine decided to create a simple accounting process that allowed me to make sure I didn't spend more money than I had coming in.

PMfP: I can see that you are a big advocate of the fourth process of project management, namely project control.

Cliff: I really am. Without having some way to examine how I spend my time and money on my business—which is really what is meant by control—I wouldn't have a business. It's as simple as that.

PMfP: Speaking of control, I'm afraid that brings us to the end of our interview. Thank you very much for your time.

Cliff: My pleasure.

CONTROLLING

Without control, the budget, schedule and scope of a project would be subject to the individual opinion of everyone associated with the project. If a project engineer felt as if the time budgeted for his/her part of the project was less than what was needed to do the job right, he/she would just spend as much time as they wanted, thereby busting the budget and schedule for that task. They would wreak havoc on the overall project timeline and the amount of project money available for other tasks.

Let's face it. Planners are not known to always meet deadlines and stay within budget constraints. We have a tendency to become so involved with our work that deadlines and financial agreements go out the window in order to "do the job right." That is all fine and good if we are the only ones affected by our casualness towards constraints. However, on planning projects, we are never really alone. Other people (and sometimes projects) are affected when we do not get our projects completed on time and within budget. Such behavior also makes it very difficult to be taken seriously the next time we agree to abide by a preset budget for a new project.

Control is an extremely important process of project management. On average, it should consume approximately 25% of our time and energies as a project manager (see Table 3-1 in Chapter 3). That may seem like a lot of time to keep track of the status of the project. However, it is an appropriate use of our time if we are going to bring our planning projects in on time, within budget and in line with our scope.

Change Control

One of the most difficult jobs of a project manager is dealing with changes to the project. At nearly every stage of the project, someone is going to want to revise the WBS or request more time or money, or an emergency will occur that requires the project manager to consider a revision. Change is to be expected and, in some cases, it can result in a better project. However, it is the project manager's responsibility to be the funnel for any changes.

A process must be established that provides the project manager and the team with some checks and balances when changes are considered. Job Aid 6-1 is an example of a simple form that can be used to organize any requested change. In order for the process of change control to be effective, the following guidelines should be followed:

- The project manager must review all changes to the project *before* they occur.
- The project manager will review the requested change and weigh the potential impact.
- If the potential impact to the project's schedule, cost or scope is relatively minor, the project manager can decide to approve the change.
- If the potential impact of the change is great, the project manager will consult with the project sponsor to determine the best course of action.
- No change to the project scope, cost or schedule can occur until the team has received an approval from the project manager.

It is the project manager's job to determine how to track and integrate any changes into the project. The tracking system may take several forms—from very complex to rather simple. If the project manager is using a sophisticated project management information system (like Primavera), change requests and actions can be tracked and organized through the information system. Unique forms can be developed and generated or the notes portion of the software can be used to keep track of the requests and subsequent events. The other end of the complexity scale might be a three-ring binder maintained by the project manager that is used to hold copies of change requests and related actions.

The important point to remember is that it is the project manager's responsibility to organize, monitor and document any requested changes to the project. It may become critical that the documentation be used to request additional people or money, or to justify a change to the project schedule. This is an area in which the project manager must be extremely disciplined and thoroughly document all change requests in order to effectively communicate with decision-makers.

Let's not forget that, with planning projects, it is often our ultimate customer—the public—that requests changes to our projects. In fact, we ask for their input during public meetings and workshops. As a result, we need to summarize their requests, identify ways to address their comments and submit the alternatives to elected officials or advisory bodies. Requests like a more detailed environmental analysis as part of a comprehensive plan, stricter landscaping requirements in a zoning ordinance, or a higher level of service for a roadway in a transportation corridor study are all examples of the types of change requests that the public may make during the execution of a planning project. The project manager must apply a change control methodology in order to deal with these requests so that a logical, fair and well-documented decision system is established.

Monitoring

Quite often, unannounced internal or external influences cause a deviation from the cost, schedule or scope of a project. In fact, these kinds of changes are to be expected. As planners, we know that it is rare when a plan is perfectly followed from beginning to end. It is the same for project plans.

Since these kinds of changes are unannounced and usually unanticipated, the project manager must have a way to know when deviations to the project plan are occurring. The project manager needs a regular monitoring and reporting system on the progress of the project plan.

The sophistication of the monitoring system will generally reflect the complexity of the project. Complex projects require complex monitoring systems; relatively simple projects can use less complex monitoring systems. However, at a minimum, computerized project tracking software of some kind should be used. As mentioned previously, Microsoft Project works well for most planning projects and has a sufficient monitoring component. Computer spreadsheets can also be developed and used by the project manager to monitor the status of the project.

The important point to remember is that the project manager must perform periodic checks between actual and planned expenditures and schedules. Every morning, the project manager should set aside an hour or so just to review progress on the project and compare the progress with the plan.

One of the best ways to check progress on the project is to ask team members. It is amazing how many project managers sit back and think, "If there are any problems, my team members will come to me." Most of the time it doesn't work that way. Unless the project manager asks, he/she is the last person to know that the project has a problem. Waiting for the team members to voluntarily share bad news is not a good strategy for controlling the project. "Management by walking around" is still one of the most reliable data-gathering methods available to managers—even project managers.

Earned Value

Earned Value (EV) is a commonly accepted method for measuring the progress of a project against the plan. It provides the project manager and team with a standard way to determine if any difference, or variance, between the current status of the project and the plan is substantial enough to take action. It is important to remember that the only time a project is perfectly in line with the project plan is before the project starts. Once the project begins, variances begin. The job of the project manager is to determine if the variance justifies any action and, if so, what action to take.

The following factors are all important to the discussion of EV:

Planned Value. Planned Value (PV), or what is sometimes called the "budgeted cost of work scheduled," is the value of the work being assessed. For example, if the project involves public meetings, and the project plan estimates the need for five public meetings with an individual cost of $1,500 (including staff time, materials and meeting room overhead) for a total cost of $7,500:

$$(5 \text{ meetings}) \times (\$1,500 \text{ per meeting})$$
$$= \$7,500 \text{ total cost planned for public meetings}$$

In this example, the PV for public meetings is $7,500. That is the amount of money the project plan anticipated spending on public meetings.

Actual Cost. The actual cost (AC), or what is sometimes called the "actual cost of work performed," is the amount of money spent on the task. In our example on public meetings, let's say we have held two meetings and each meeting costs $2,000:

$$(2 \text{ meetings}) \times (\$2,000 \text{ per meeting}) = \$4,000 \text{ spent on meetings}$$

This is a fairly simple example, so it is clear that we are on the road to having a problem. We have already spent $4,000 of our budgeted $7,500 and we have three more meetings to hold. Intuitively, we know there is a problem, but how do we communicate that to our team and decision-makers? What standard do we use on this potential cost overrun? This is when the concept of EV comes into play.

Earned Value. EV provides us with a commonly accepted method for discussing the status of a project. EV, also known as the "budgeted cost of work performed," estimates the value of the work performed. In our example, we have completed two of the five meetings, or 40% of the planned work. The total cost of public meetings was planned at $7,500. Therefore, the EV for the meetings is $3,000:

$$40\% \text{ (2 of 5 meetings completed)}$$
$$\times \$7,500 \text{ (total cost of meetings planned)}$$
$$= \$3,000 \text{ (EV)}$$

EV tells us that, according to our plan, we should have spent $3,000 on the two meetings, not $4,000. It is clear that we have a problem with which we will need to deal. We are on the path of blowing our public meeting budget.

Cost Variance. The Cost Variance (CV) simply measures the difference between what we planned to spend on a task (PV) and what we have actually spent (AC). In our example the CV is -$1,000:

$$PV (\$3,000) - AC (\$4,000) = CV (-\$1,000)$$

A negative CV indicates a potential problem and a positive CV tells us that we are on the right track. It is a simple way to convey the financial status of the project.

We have used a fairly simple example to explain EV. In reality, calculating an accurate EV—especially for planning projects—can be a very difficult job. Preparing planning projects is not like building widgets on an assembly line. We don't manufacture plans in the same way as we do paper clips.

It is very difficult to measure the percent complete of a planning project. Is the draft zoning ordinance 20% complete or 45% complete? The difference can mean a great deal to the EV calculation. In our example, we used the number of meetings completed as a measure of the percent complete of our public meeting project task. This assumes that all of the five meetings are equal in effort and complexity. Again, reality

Estimating Percent Complete

A project manager must determine the percent complete of tasks in a planning project in order to control the progress of the project. Estimating percent complete is difficult because no two planning projects are exactly alike. If they were exactly alike, project managers would know precisely how to measure every step of a planning project. With that in mind, there are some ways to estimate percent complete that provide a degree of accuracy.

• *Experience.* Men and women who have years of experience have a great deal to offer when estimating percent complete. These are the "go to people" for a project manager. A wise project manager will ask experienced staff for their input and opinion in estimating the percent complete of a task or project. The "gray beards" have learned a lot of lessons in their time regardless of where they are in the organization, and a good project manager will seek them out for feedback.

• *Trends.* All project managers need to keep track of how much work has been accomplished. It is not important whether this is accomplished through formal reports by the project team or by the project manager walking around and informally chatting with the team for a few minutes every day or two. The important thing for the project manager is to receive regular feedback from team members on how far along they think they are in completing their task. *Remember:* this does not involve how much time or money they have spent on the task, but rather what percentage of the overall task they think they have completed. With this information, the project manager can determine any troubling patterns or trends in the completion of a task.

• *Past Projects.* Another good method for estimating percent complete of planning projects is consulting past project records or managers. In some cases, history can be a good predictor of the future. Contacting previous project managers of similar projects and asking them what to keep an eye on or how to estimate percent completes is an excellent technique. In addition, records from past projects can also provide insight to the planning project manager on what to look for when determining percent complete.

has taught us that this assumption is probably not true. However, it is important to make an estimate on how much of the overall task we think is completed.

EV is an excellent tool to assist the project manager in controlling his/her project. An important point to remember is to not get too carried away with the EV concept. It is an excellent tool and one that planning project managers must adopt to ensure that their projects do not go over budget or off schedule. However, as with any report or calculation, EV can be misleading unless the project manager also consults with the project team members. A five-minute conversation with a key planner on a project can often provide more information than a five-page status report. *Don't forget to talk with team members.* They are the real experts on how the project is progressing and what time bombs may exist.

Project Adjustments

Controlling the project also means responding to problems identified by the status reports. The project may be behind schedule or over budget. What should the project manager do? What are his/her options?

Two methods for dealing with scheduling and budget issues are fast tracking and crashing. These are two tools a project manager can use if changes need to be made. Both options should be used only after careful consideration and after a problem has been clearly established.

Fast Tracking. Fast tracking occurs when time needs to be made up on a project. It simply means running two or more tasks in parallel to accelerate the schedule. Fast tracking is a simple concept and, on many projects, is easy to carry out. However, on more complex projects, the project manager should assess the potential impact of fast tracking before choosing to implement. Things to consider include:

• *What tasks are independent of each other and can be run concurrently?* The WBS is a great source to consult when answering this question.

• *Do we have the staff to fast track?* Some tasks may have been scheduled sequentially because the same person or people were going to work on them. Fast tracking requires two separate teams to work on two separate tasks at the same time. Physics has taught us that the same person cannot be in two places, doing two different things, at the same time.

• *What are the impacts to other tasks?* Usually the project tasks were scheduled a certain way for a reason. Fast tracking can have scheduling and resource consequences extending into many other tasks. Will the project team be able to take advantage of two or more tasks being completed at or near the same time? Will the team have the resources to begin subsequent tasks once the fast-tracked tasks are completed?

Crashing. Crashing a project involves putting more resources on a project without directly changing the WBS dependencies. A project manager crashes a project when he/she needs to speed it up. Crashing also has issues to consider prior to deciding to go forward:

- *Are resources available?* Crashing involves adding unplanned additional resources—usually people—to a project. This assumes that the resources are available. A project manager must be wary of throwing any warm body on a project. Additional team members must have the needed skills and talents required to complete the tasks. Otherwise, the project could actually be delayed due to inexperienced or unproductive staff.

- *What is the cost of crashing?* Crashing involves more cost. Adding resources means spending more money. There is no way around it. The project manager must determine whether or not the project can absorb or take on the additional costs associated with crashing.

- *What is the impact of crashing on team members?* A project team is a cohesive unit. Adding resources—or people—to a team can be positive or negative. The project manager's job is to ensure that it is a positive experience. If there is no positive outcome from crashing, it should not occur.

When assessing these questions, the project manager is well advised to use project management software to address these "what if" questions regarding fast tracking and crashing (assuming that the WBS, timelines and resources were loaded into the project management computer program).

Various scenarios can be run through the software to assess potential impacts of running parallel tasks (fast tracking) or adding more resources (crashing) to a project. The ability to run scenarios and examine the implications *before* making these important decisions is one of the major reasons for taking the time to load a project into a computer tracking program. Unplanned and undesirable consequences can be avoided by using a computer as a guinea pig instead of the project team.

The potential for unintended consequences is huge when making project adjustments like fast tracking or crashing a project. The impacts of changing schedules or resources on a project may not be realized for weeks or even months; however, once the changes have been made, they cannot be taken back.

Imagine having to renegotiate additional time for several team members with their functional line manager only to find out that they are not available. Do you remember what it was like going back to the city council asking for more money on a project? Just think of the look in the public's eyes when you tell them that a deadline for a neighborhood plan is going to be delayed. These are not fun things to do and should be considered only after the project manager has investigated all alternatives and scenarios and has determined that there are no other courses of action.

At a minimum, the project manager must consult with the project sponsors once a need to alter a project has been identified. The project manager should bring two or three alternative solutions to the sponsors with a recommended course of action. If at all possible, this should occur before taking the action. The project manager should get the sponsor's buy-in on the changes prior to them taking place.

Advance notice should also be given to, and input gathered from, interested and affected parties before major project changes are made. If outside parties are given a chance to become familiar with and provide comments on changes to a planning project before the changes are made, they will feel like true partners in the project, not simply a nuisance with which they must deal. If a project manager can show the alternatives and the consequences of each alternative, the parties will begin to understand the difficulties and complexities of project management. This understanding will go a long ways towards getting their ultimate acceptance of the final plan.

Weekly Progress Reports

Weekly progress reports are an excellent way to keep project sponsors, team members and interested and affected members of the public aware of how the project is progressing. The reports do not need to be lengthy, complex documents. In fact, they should be short, simple to read and to the point; the less technical, the better. The purpose of the progress report is to communicate, not obfuscate.

At a minimum, the weekly progress reports should contain a Gantt chart or something similar (see Figure 4-5 in Chapter 4) showing the progress and schedule for completion of the project's major tasks. This visual aid can go a long way towards communicating the status of the project in a manner that everyone can understand.

The weekly progress report should also include:

• *Work Completed in the Last Week.* This is a brief narrative on the specific tasks or individual work that the team accomplished since the last report.

• *Status of Major Tasks.* This is a short description of the Gantt chart indicating which tasks are on schedule and which tasks, if any, are behind schedule. If any of the tasks are behind schedule, it is important to explain why they are not on schedule and any course of action the project manager anticipates taking to bring them in on time.

• *Constraints/Opportunities.* This is an opportunity for the project manager to briefly describe any internal or external influences that might affect the project in the near future. Issues such as unplanned events (like storms or power outages) or equipment failures are examples of constraints that may affect a plan.

• *Planned Work.* It is important to let the readers of the report know what work is anticipated to be accomplished over the next week.

Weekly progress reports are a necessary step for a project manager. They are especially important for planning projects that receive close scrutiny by elected officials and the public. As mentioned earlier, the weekly reports do not need to be lengthy tomes that take several days to complete. They should be brief and factual. A project manager should plan to spend an hour or two a week preparing progress reports, which will be time well spent. Job Aid 6-2 offers an outline for a weekly progress report.

REVIEW

• Approximately 25% of a project manager's time should be spent on controlling the project.

• Change control establishes a process for dealing with anticipated requests and unanticipated issues that may affect the schedule, cost or scope of a project.

• Project management software provides the project manager with an excellent tool for monitoring and reporting the status of a project.

- A good project manager will use the "management by walking around" technique to stay in touch with the project team.
- EV is an excellent method to objectively gauge actual work accomplished against the project plan to determine if the project is on schedule.
- Every planning project will require adjustments sometime during execution. Fast tracking and crashing are two techniques to get a lagging project back on track.
- The nature of planning projects demands that weekly progress reports be prepared by the project manager to keep the project sponsors, team members, elected officials, and affected and interested members of the public informed on the status of the project.

Job Aid 6-1. Change Request Form

Project Name:
Person Requesting the Change:
Tasks Affected by the Change (from the WBS):
Brief Description of the Change:
Potential Impact of the Change on the Project's Scope, Schedule and Cost:
Recommended Course of Action:
Signature of the Person Requesting the Change: Date:
Project Manager's Signature: Date:

Job Aid 6-2. Weekly Progress Report

Project Name:	
Project Manager:	Reporting Period:
Work Completed in Past Week:	
Status of Major Tasks:	
Constraints/Opportunities:	
Work Planned for Next Week:	
Project Manager's Signature:	Date:

RESOURCES

Kerzner, Harold. *Project Management: A Systems Approach to Planning, Scheduling, and Controlling, 7*th *Ed.* New York, NY: John Wiley & Sons, 2000.

Project Management Software. Web site: http://www.oneanthem.com/home.nsf

7

Closing

To make a long story short, there's nothing like having a boss walk in.

—DORIS LILLY

It takes less time to do a thing right, than it does to explain why you did it wrong.

—HENRY WADSWORTH LONGFELLOW

There are two kinds of people, those who finish what they start and so on ...

—ROBERT BYRNE

INTERVIEW

PMfP interviewed Karl Kastle on the subject of closing a project. Karl was born and raised in California and has spent most of his 12 years of planning experience in that state. He has a checkered past when it comes to managing planning projects. Some of his projects have been successful and others have not. Karl has learned a lot from his mistakes.

PMfP: Karl, we understand that you have had some problem projects.

Karl: Yes, that's true. I'm not batting one thousand when it comes to managing projects.

PMfP: Sometimes we learn more from our mistakes than our successes. Tell us about some of the lessons you have learned.

Karl: One of the lessons I've learned is to not assume that everyone involved with a project has the same ultimate goal as you.

PMfP: What do you mean?

Karl: I mean that, as a project manager on various planning projects, I had the goal of producing quality products on time and within budget. Some people have a real problem with that concept.

PMfP: You mean some individuals involved with projects don't want to bring in a well-designed and well-written plan?

Karl: I'm no psychiatrist, but it seems to me that there are some project team members and members of the public who have a real problem with finishing things. It's as if they are frightened of completing the project because they aren't sure what they will do next. It's very bizarre.

PMfP: That is bizarre. I don't think I have ever heard that before.

Karl: It has certainly been an eye-opener for me. I have managed projects where the most difficult part of my job was getting the project team and some members of the public to agree to complete the project. I have literally had to turn a planner's computer off to get him to stop writing the environmental section of a plan. The man was scared to death of finishing his portion of the plan. I can understand it if someone doesn't like what the plan says or recommends and they want to make revisions, but I'm talking about something different. I'm talking about a kind of phobia about wrapping up the final deliverable.

PMfP: I can see where that would pose a problem.

Karl: You might say that. The whole purpose of a project is to produce a final product or deliverable. If you can't get a team to quit working on a deliverable, it will never get delivered.

PMfP: So how do you deal with this problem?

Karl: For one thing, I get everyone to agree up front on what the final product will look like and when it is scheduled for completion. That can go a long way towards fighting off the desire by some people to keep refining the project. This may sound a little strange, but I also assure the team members that they are valued and have another exciting project awaiting them. If they understand that they have to complete their current project before they can begin a new one, they are more motivated to wrap up and move on.

PMfP: That's very helpful. What else have you learned?

Karl: To do what you are doing here with me. To debrief, or in other words, to discuss and document "lessons learned" from a project.

PMfP: How do you do that and why?

Karl: First of all, I conduct a "lessons learned" session so that I don't repeat the same mistakes twice. If we take the time to review what went well and what didn't go so well on a project, we are less likely to repeat the mistakes. It also reinforces the things we did well so that we repeat those on future projects.

PMfP: How do you do "lessons learned"?

Karl: I like to have a big pizza party after the final deliverable is completed. I try to make it a fun event so that people are more open to discuss what didn't go well on the project. I invite everyone on the team, especially the administrative assistants. The secretaries are the ones who usually take the brunt of project problems and are just waiting to be asked about them. They are a wealth of information. A word of caution: I always tell the team that they will not be harmed by anything that is said in the debriefing sessions. In other words, identifying or admitting a mistake will not result in any disciplinary action against them. Once they understand that, the floodgates open and the learning about how to improve the next project really takes place.

PMfP: I want to thank you for your insight on how to close a project. Our discussion has been very insightful.

Karl: I'm glad to pass along some of what I've learned so that others won't have to repeat my mistakes.

CLOSING

Closing a project is a process of project management that is often ignored or minimized. While it is not intended to be as lengthy and resource-consuming as Planning or Executing, it should be well thought out and performed. On average, closing out a project takes approximately 10% of the project manager's overall time and energy (see Table 3-1 in Chapter 3).

A major aspect of closing a project involves ensuring that the customers are satisfied with the final product. For planning projects, this means consulting with the project sponsors, elected officials and the public. Based on the input from these sources, the project manager must make a decision on whether to revise the scope of the planning project to address these concerns or complete the project. If the project manager and team decide to complete the project, the final product must be turned over to the end users.

As mentioned by Karl in our interview, closing the project also includes taking a little time to review what went well on the project and what could be improved on the next project. This can be a career-enhancing effort for the project manager and team. The team must also transition from the "old" project to the "new" project. Acknowledging that this transition must take place, and planning for it, can make the process much less painful.

The final step in closing out a project is archiving the project data and documents. This is important for any project, but especially important for planning projects. Plans are public documents and, by their very nature, must be open to challenges and inquiries. Since, in most cases, the plans were funded by public money, the public has a right to learn as much about the rationale behind a plan's recommendations as possible. Properly archiving the information that went into the plan's recommendations can prevent a lot of legal and ethical challenges later on.

Customer Sign-off

Every planning project has a customer and end-user base. These are the groups and individuals that requested the plan or will be influenced by its outcome. Planning projects usually have a rather large customer base. We addressed customers and stakeholders in Chapter 3. These are the people that must be consulted when the project is complete.

Below are a couple of points to remember when seeking customer sign-off of a planning project.

Primary Customers. When asking customers to sign off on the final project deliverable, the Quadrant I customers and stakeholders (see Figure 3-1 in Chapter 3) should be the primary focus. These are the people that are amenable to reason and have a high ability to influence the outcome. Once the Quadrant I group has agreed to accept the final plan, the potential for the final plan to be considered acceptable is greatly enhanced.

Items to Defer. When discussing the acceptance of the final deliverable, it is usually appropriate to discuss items that can be deferred until the next plan update. This is a good time to review the Project Charter, the project plan and the WBS. The customers were consulted when these products were prepared, but sometimes they will have forgotten some of the details and rationale behind the project plan by the time the project is complete. Many times the individual players will have changed, such as elected officials. If this is the case, the project manager and sponsors should review the work and assumptions that originally went into defining the plan. The project manager's job at these discussions is to either get the customers to accept the plan as is, to identify items to defer, or to negotiate a new scope, more time and/or additional resources.

Progress, Not Perfection. An important concept to remember is "progress, not perfection." Is the final deliverable good enough? It is fine to always strive for perfection; however, few of our plans will ever be perfect. During the close-out of a planning project, we must determine if it is good enough to finish now, recognizing that there will always be another day to plan.

Sometimes the project team is the most difficult group of people to convince that a project is good enough. As we mentioned earlier, planners are perfectionists. We like to do it right the first time. The determination of whether a project deliverable is good enough to accept is really another way of defining what is right. This is when the team and the customer must understand that a decision to not accept the deliverable has consequences. The result of not accepting the final deliverable will mean more time, more money or a revised scope. It is the project manager's job to communicate the alternatives—and the consequences of the alternatives—to the project team and customers. Ultimately, they must make the final decision; however, it must be a fully informed decision.

Turning Over the Final Product

At this point, the deliverable is complete, all input has been received and the customer has signed off. This is when the final and complete product is turned over to the customer. Turning over the final product seems like such a simple concept—and it is, if done correctly. However, if the project is not properly turned over to the customer by the project manager, months and months of hard work by the team can be diminished.

When receiving the final product, the customer must acknowledge receipt and completeness of the deliverable. Think of this process as the final walk-through when buying a house. Just before closing on the purchase of a new house, the buyer and realtor perform a final inspection of the property. This is done so that the buyer can be assured that no last-minute changes were made by the owner just before the sale. The buyer wants to make sure that all of the stipulations of the sales contract have been met. If the contract says that the house will contain a washer/dryer and the curtains stay, the buyer wants to make sure that they are in the house at closing.

The final walk-through at the sale of a house also protects the realtor and seller. They review the contract, confirm with the buyer that they

Handing Over a Deliverable

Following are a couple of pointers to remember when handing over a deliverable to the customer:

• *Packaging.* The visual impression of the final product can have a tremendous impact on how it is received. Even if the project scope does not include packaging tasks, it is a good idea to spend a little time and money to make the product look professional. Depending on the size and scope of the project, this may mean three-ring binders with color cover inserts, or an elaborate Web site with an accompanying CD-ROM including graphics, sound and video clips.

• *Signature.* Don't forget to get the signature from the customer (or their representative) on the final deliverable. The process of actually signing a document can help eliminate questions or even legal challenges down the road.

• *Public Celebration.* Part of the fun of working on and completing a planning project is that it is a public document. Public documents belong to the public. When a plan is complete, it is appropriate to have a celebration. The celebration may be a formal signing ceremony by the elected officials. The signing ceremony may take place in the city/county chambers or, even better, out at the planning site. The celebration may also include something resembling more of a street party or ribbon-cutting ceremony. However it is accomplished, it is important to remember to celebrate the completion of the project. It helps to recognize a job well done and bring closure for the team and public.

still agree with the stipulations and that the stipulations have been met. The buyer inspects the house and agrees to close on the house. The final walk-through inspection is usually a formality since all of the professional inspections and major stipulations have been met by the time of the walk-through.

Handing the final project deliverable to the customer is very similar to the final walk-through inspection before buying a house, except that the final deliverable from a planning project has usually cost more than an average new home. The project team has invested a lot of time, money and sweat in the preparation of the final deliverable—not to mention the amount of volunteer hours spent by community groups and elected or appointed officials. The importance of properly turning over a planning project deliverable should not be minimized. Job Aid 7-1 presents a project completion sign-off checklist to assist with this process.

Lessons Learned

The natural urge after completing one project is to take a short break and then begin working on another one. Most team members want to smell the roses for a few days after a long project. This is understandable and should be allowed. However, there is one more project task that must be completed after the deliverable has been delivered before the project is truly finished.

The project manager must schedule and facilitate a "lessons learned" session with the project team. The session does not need to be more than three to four hours long. The important point is to just *do it*. Getting people to attend the session could be one of the most difficult things a project manager ever does. Usually, the last thing the team wants to do is discuss the project that they have just completed. They want to move on to another new and exciting project.

If the "lessons learned" session is run properly, it can be fun and informative. When holding the meeting, the project manager should consider the following:

- *Serve food.* Serving food can go a long way towards getting people to show up and making the meeting tolerable.

- *Discuss problems.* Talking about what went wrong is the easy part of the meeting. This is the time when people vent their frustrations and difficulties, which are still fresh on their minds.

- *Acknowledge the things that went well.* This is often overlooked. It shouldn't be taken for granted.

- *Invite administrative assistants.* They have a tremendous amount of insight and will be pleased to share it, if asked.

- *Ask the team how they would improve the next project.* They will have tremendous insight in ways that the project manager and team can make the next project even better. Use them.

- *Invite customers and members of the public.* This can go a long way towards establishing credibility with the community and learning from their perspective. This is particularly true for planning projects that are in the public's view.

- *Make sure the meeting is well documented.* The notes from the meeting will be very valuable in future projects to help minimize mistakes and duplicate the successes.

- *Thank the team for their hard work.* They are the ones that made the project a success.

Job Aid 7-2 provides a sample agenda for the "lessons learned" meeting. After the meeting is conducted, a short summary of the conclusions and recommendations should be written and shared with everyone on the team. In most cases, the lessons learned from your project will help other project teams. The point is to learn from our mistakes and successes regardless of who is the project team or manager. This is a tremendous opportunity for the entire organization to take a forward step in professionalism.

Team Transitions

Once a team has completed a project, the members must move on to new projects. The concept of transition from one project to another is important for the project manager to understand.

Several of the items discussed in this chapter fall under the category of team transitions. Turning over the final product and conducting "lessons learned" sessions begin the transition process from the old project to the new one. In many cases, team members will be working on more than one project at a time, so there may not be a clear and distinct end of one project coinciding with the beginning of a new project.

The process of project transition should be acknowledged and followed to facilitate the team members' progression to new work. Having a party to celebrate the conclusion of a project is a nice way to say "job well done." Team members' performance should be recognized along with major accomplishments. It is time to kick back and appreciate a finished product.

It is also a good time to mend any fences and rebuild bridges that may have suffered during the heat of the project. More than likely, the team members will be working together again on a future project. It does no good to have festering resentments carry over into a new project. The transition process is an excellent way to end a project on a positive note so that new work can begin in a productive manner.

Document Archiving

Archiving documents from planning projects is especially important for several reasons. First, planning projects are living documents that are periodically updated. They are rarely completed, put on the shelf and never again consulted. Plans are implemented, updated and revised on a regular basis. This aspect of planning projects requires that the supporting documentation that went into the development of the project be readily accessible after the project has been completed.

Many state planning statutes require that local government comprehensive plans be updated every three to five years. In order to do so, the supporting documentation and background work that went into development of the original plan should be available to the team charged with updating the plan. Otherwise, the team updating the plan will need to start from scratch, which is expensive and time-consuming. In addition, the plan update may not be based on the same data and assumptions that built the original plan, thereby making the update inaccurate or unacceptable to the public.

Another reason for archiving the documents for planning projects is that, unfortunately, plans are sometimes legally challenged. When a plan is brought to court, the group that developed the plan must be able to defend the plan and its recommendations. The team that put the plan together must, in essence, be able to duplicate the work that went into writing the plan. This requires that the team be able to put their hands on the original data, supporting documents and summaries of public input that established the basis for the plan's recommendations and conclusions.

When a team is able to show the original data and supporting documentation that went into developing the plan, they have a much greater chance of having it upheld in court. Having easily accessible, archived documentation can be the difference between a plan that is legally standing and one that is required by the courts to be revised or thrown out entirely.

Archiving the project documents simply means keeping the original hard copy and electronic versions of material that were used in the development of the project. In concept, it is an easy task; in reality, properly archiving large amounts of information can be difficult and expensive.

The task of archiving a project will depend on the size and complexity of the project. The larger the project, the more complex the task of archiving documents. Properly archiving the project's documents may require purchasing additional computer storage capabilities or using a professional document retrieval company.

A log of the documents indicating the content, date and size of the material should be developed and kept in a central area, usually the planning department. Every time one of the documents is taken, the log should be signed to indicate who took the document and when they removed it from the archive. Being able to track down who has the information can be very important if the plan is challenged in court. It can also make the process of updating the planning project much more efficient.

REVIEW

- Closing out a project is an important step that can easily be overlooked.
- Approximately 10% of the overall time of a project manager is spent closing out a project.
- Having the customer review and sign off on the final project deliverable is the first step in closing out a project.
- Questions to consider when having the customer sign off on the deliverable are: Who are the primary customers? Which items can be deferred? When can the final product be determined as "good to go"?
- After the customer has reviewed the final product and determined that it is complete according to the agreed-upon scope of services, the project manager must arrange for the complete deliverable to be turned over to the customer.
- "Lessons learned" is the process of having the team and affected parties identify the aspects of the project that went well and should be repeated, and acknowledge those things that did not go well and should never be done again.
- Every closing process on every project should include "lessons learned."
- Assisting the team in transitioning from the "old" project to the "new" project is something that the project manager should anticipate and carry out.
- Properly archiving documents is critical for planning projects in order to facilitate updates and defend legal challenges.

Job Aid 7-1. Project Completion Sign-off Checklist

Approved (✔)	Person/Entity	Date
	Project Manager	
	Project Team	
	Project Sponsor	
	Elected Officials	
	Neighborhood Groups	
	Advisory Boards	

Job Aid 7-2. Agenda for "Lessons Learned" Meeting

I.	Welcome and Congratulations
II.	What Went Well
III.	What Did Not Go Well
IV.	Ways to Improve
V.	Thank You
VI.	Adjourn

RESOURCE

Mens, Rob and Howyi Nelson. "Best Practices: Big Projects Succeed in a Small Town" *PM Network*, December 2000, pp. 35-37.

3

Case Studies and Perspectives

Part 3 of this book provides the reader with two final chapters. Chapter 8 consists of four case studies. Each case study describes a planning project, its deliverables and lessons learned from the project. The focus of these case studies is on the application of project management principles in planning projects. The projects represent a range of complexities and perspectives. These are all descriptions of real projects.

Chapter 9 wraps up the subject of project management for planners by offering important nontechnical suggestions for project managers to remember. These perspectives are the product of years of experience managing planning projects. It is hoped that planners can use these suggestions to move beyond current obstacles and progress the planning profession even further.

8

Case Studies

What counts is not necessarily the size of the dog in the fight, but the size of the fight in the dog.

—DWIGHT D. EISENHOWER

Character may be manifested in the great moments, but it is made in the small ones.

—PHILLIPS BROOKS

In this day and age, if you're not confused, you're not thinking clearly.

—BURT MANNIS

INTRODUCTION

This chapter provides a glimpse of real-world applications of the project management approach on planning projects. The projects chosen include a mix of planning projects and customers. By doing so, it is hoped that the reader is given a broad perspective of how the processes of project management can provide planners with a framework for completing quality planning projects on time and within budget.

Not all of the projects described in this chapter are shining examples of project management principles at work. In at least one case, experience shows what *not* to do. Sometimes we learn more from our mistakes than from our successes. In one case, the project manager learned a great deal about what not to repeat on his next planning project.

Each case study is divided into three sections: Background, Deliverables and Lessons Learned. The case studies are not intended to be

111

exhaustive studies of the subject projects; to do so is beyond the scope of this book. The purpose of the project write-ups is to give the reader a look at project management theory in practice. The Lessons Learned section of each case study details what the project manager and team believed went well on the project and what did not go so well.

CASE STUDY #1: SAVING THE EVERGLADES

Background

Between 1995 and 1999, the U.S. Army Corps of Engineers (Corps) and the South Florida Water Management District (District) developed a plan for the restoration of the Everglades (see Figure 8-1) while providing for the other water-related needs of the region, including water supply and flood protection. This plan, known as the Comprehensive Everglades Restoration Plan (CERP), sets out an extensive program of projects designed to meet an aggressive set of goals and objectives to save the Everglades.

The CERP is arguably the world's largest environmental restoration program. It covers a planning area from Orlando through the Keys (see Figure 8-2). The current permanent population for the area is approximately 6.5 million and is expected to double during the life of the plan. This area of south Florida also has one of the most productive agricultural regions in the country, producing winter vegetables, sugar cane and citrus.

The restoration plan centers on an update of the region's water management system known as the Central and Southern Florida (C&SF) Project. This network of more than 1,000 miles of canals, 720 miles of levees, and several hundred water control structures and pump stations has provided water supply, flood control and other water management benefits to the region for 50 years. The objective of the CERP is to redesign the C&SF Project to provide clean water to the Everglades in the right amount at the right time, ensure a safe and reliable source of water to the urban and agricultural communities, and provide flood protection to the region now and in the future.

Following are some important aspects of the CERP:

- The Corps and the District were co-sponsors of the project and equally shared the expense of developing the CERP.
- Each agency had a project manager and team members working on the development of the CERP.

Figure 8-1. The Everglades

Figure 8-2. CERP Planning Region

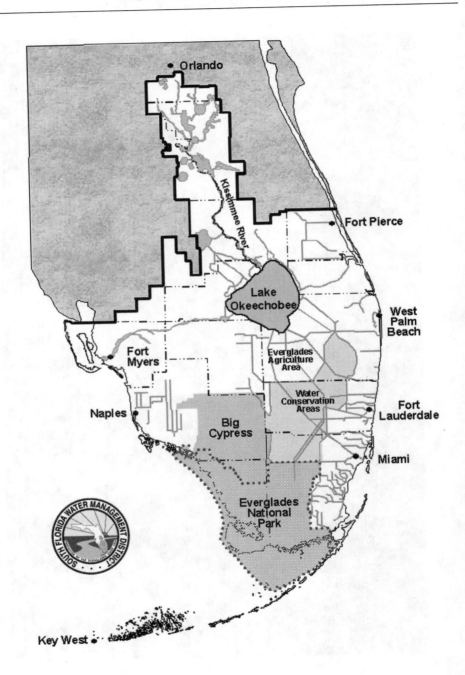

• The project team was interdisciplinary, including planners, engineers, biologists, ecologists, economists, hydrologists, modelers, real estate specialists, public outreach specialists and resource managers.

• The Corps and the District each had a distinct and different organizational culture, financial and time accounting system and approach to project management.

• The local Corps offices are in Jacksonville, Florida and the District's headquarters are in West Palm Beach, Florida—over 250 miles apart.

• A Reconnaissance Study was completed in 1994 that described in detail the primary objectives of the CERP.

• More than 30 agencies and a series of numerous public meetings provided input to the development of the CERP.

• Stakeholders included: public and private water utilities; local, state and federal agencies and elected officials; two Native American tribes; agribusiness; land developers; and nonprofit environmental interest groups.

• The CERP project began in 1995 and was completed in 1999 when it was sent to the United States Congress for review and approval.

Deliverables

The final CERP project deliverables consisted of a 500-page plan and 3,000 pages of appendices. When the plan was being developed, a unique interactive Web site was created that allowed any visitor to perform alternative analyses presenting engineering modeling results from a series of potential implementation options.

The final plan approved by Congress includes 68 components consisting of construction projects. The estimated cost of implementing the CERP project is $7.8 billion, with $175 million needed each year for maintenance, operation and monitoring.

Lessons Learned

The CERP project team went through a formal process of identifying and discussing lessons learned from the project. Many of the same people that were on the project team for the CERP are on the team that is coordinating the implementation of the restoration plan. They will be working together to manage and coordinate the construction of the projects recommended by the CERP. Since many of the same team members will be working together on implementation, they have a real vested interest in identifying the ways to improve their team. Following are lessons learned as identified by the CERP project team:

• *Team Size and Make-Up.* The project team for development of the CERP was large and included a wide variety of professionals. This proved to be both a strength and a weakness. It was a strength because the different professional perspectives provided a wide spectrum of interests and knowledge areas. Each professional on the team brought his/her own view on the goals and design of the plan. This diverse outlook ensured that all views were addressed in the plan. The large number of team members and their differing views of what the plan should address was also a weakness because it made decision-making time-consuming and, at times, frustrating. The team was rarely able to quickly agree on an issue and move forward. The project managers from the Corps and the District managed the team meetings and tried to be inclusive in hearing differing opinions. This made it difficult to come to consensus on tough issues.

• *Use a third-party coordinator/facilitator to run the team meetings.* That person would be perceived as neutral by the team and could work with all individual members to arrive at agreement more quickly.

• *Ensure that all external stakeholders are involved in the planning process inception.* The project team felt that it was beneficial to have received input from these stakeholders early in the project.

• *Continue team-building exercises throughout the planning project.* The team went through extensive team-building exercises early in the project. However, the project took years to complete and there was turnover on the team. The negative impacts associated with the long timeline of the project and the turnover could have been minimized by carrying out team-building exercises on a regular basis throughout the life of the project.

• *Maintain a high standard and an open approach to the public.* By the end of the project, the team was repeating the phrase, "Once you start planning in a fishbowl, you can never go back." From the beginning, the CERP team operated in the public's eye. Meetings were advertised and the citizens and interested parties were invited to participate. Preliminary data and draft documents were made available to the public as soon as they were drafted. The team believed that this open approach was the right thing to do and would ultimately contribute to the plan's success. They set a high standard in this regard early on. Once that standard was set, the public expected and demanded that the team continue in this manner throughout the life of the project. As a result of this open approach, the public benefited by being involved, the team benefited by learning different perspectives and the final deliverable benefited by its comprehensiveness.

CASE STUDY #2: THE LITTLE TOWN THAT COULD

Background

Pahokee is a small, rural town on the east shore of Lake Okeechobee in south Florida (see Figure 8-3). It has a permanent population of approximately 7,000 and is home to a large number of migrant farm workers who labor in sugar cane and vegetable fields near the town. Pahokee means "Grassy Waters" in the language of the Seminole Indians, who were one of the original inhabitants of the area.

In 1985, the State of Florida passed a statewide local government planning initiative that required all cities and counties in the state to write and adopt comprehensive plans. The plans had to be developed according to specific guidelines written by the state and were to be adopted by a specific date established by law. The state also allocated monies to provide to local governments for the development of their comprehensive plans.

The town's residents elected a new mayor and city council that ran on a platform of local economic growth through strong planning. The town's new mayor was a woman in her seventies who was born and raised in Pahokee. She was a powerhouse of enthusiasm and drive packed into a 5-foot frame and little more than 100 pounds.

The "Little Mayor," as she was affectionately known, and her newly elected council hired the city's first full-time planner and a planning consulting firm to prepare the city's first comprehensive plan. The project in this case study is the comprehensive plan. Characteristics of the project included the following:

• The consultant's contract with the city and the state's detailed requirements for local government comprehensive plans constituted the project scope. These two documents clearly described the deliverables that were to be completed, and the tasks that the consultant and city staff would be responsible to complete to produce the deliverables.

• Pahokee had no additional funds other than the state's planning grants to prepare the comprehensive plan. The consultant's contracted

Figure 8-3. An Aerial View of Pahokee

amount equaled the grant from the state, which totaled approximately $20,000 over two years.

- The city council, through leadership from the Little Mayor, convinced the local citizens and business community that their best hope for economic redevelopment of Pahokee was through the creation of a complete and progressive comprehensive plan. They became the city's strongest planning advocates.
- The Little Mayor, the city council and the citizens in open, advertised, public meetings reviewed preliminary drafts of all planning data and documents.

Deliverables

The City of Pahokee adopted its first comprehensive plan as a result of this project. The plan was found to meet all of the state planning requirements and, more importantly, it provided a blueprint for future economic development activities that are still going on today in the city. After the plan was completed, the city—with the help of the same consultant—went on to prepare and adopt a series of land development regulations that complemented the goals and objectives of the comprehensive plan.

Lessons Learned

- *Prepare a detailed project scope.* The project would not have been successful without the preparation of a detailed project scope. The project scope was the document to which the city, the consultant and the local community continuously referred during the preparation of the plan. It provided direction and guidance through a process that the city and citizens had never gone through before. The scope was also an excellent tool for reality checks to focus energies on the most important tasks for the city to achieve its goals.
- *Prepare an aggressive, progressive and effective planning project.* A planning project can be prepared that meets mandated requirements and yet is aggressive, progressive and effective without spending a lot of money. The city had very little money to spend on the project, yet they produced a product of which the entire community could be proud.
- *Build a project team that is fully committed to success.* You can't ignore zeal, energy and drive. What the city lacked in financial resources, they made up for in pure, unbridled passion. Through the

leadership and enthusiasm of the Little Mayor, her city council and the local community, great things were accomplished. The best project scope in the world could not be fulfilled unless the project team is fully committed to its success.

CASE STUDY #3: A SUB, IS A SUB, IS A SUB . . .

Background

This is an example of a project gone awry. An electric utility in north Florida initiated a project to expand and diversify one of its power plants. To do so, the proposed expansion had to, among other things, be approved by the state's utility commission and receive permits from the Florida Department of Environmental Protection.

The permitting and approval process is very time-consuming and exhaustive. A far-reaching plan must be prepared outlining in detail the proposed expansion and impacts to the surrounding urban communities, including an extensive environmental impact statement (EIS).

The utility company hired a large engineering consulting firm (the prime contractor) to lead the permitting and approval process. That firm in turn hired a second engineering consulting company (one of several subcontractors) to lead the EIS preparation. The second consulting company engaged the services of a third, much smaller, environmental engineering and planning firm (the subcontractor to the subcontractor) to prepare the supporting land use inventory and socio-economic analysis. The focus of this case study is on this third-level consulting firm and the project for which it was responsible. For the purposes of this book, this "sub to a sub" consulting company will be known as SOL, Inc.

The project scope for the various levels of work could be described as follows:

- *Prime Contractor.* The prime contractor had an open-ended agreement with the utility company to successfully steer the proposed power plant expansion through the permitting and approval process. The tasks were generally defined with the ultimate deliverable identified as state approval.

- *Subcontractors.* The "subs" on this project had very detailed, deliverable-oriented project scopes, defining tasks, levels of effort and costs. The prime contractor was experienced in this kind of work, and did an excellent job in preparing a useful and realistic scope for the subcontractors.

- *The Subcontractor to the Subcontractor.* SOL, Inc. had very little in writing from the subcontractor in the way of a scope for their work. They were basically asked to "handle it"—to prepare the land use inventory and socioeconomic analysis for the EIS. They were given a lump-sum amount of money to produce this work.

SOL, Inc. prepared a general project scope for internal use that outlined the tasks and milestones for its portion of the work. This project represented a major piece of work for the small firm and they wanted to do a good job. Unfortunately, there was very little communication between SOL, Inc. and the subcontractor for which they were working. The larger engineering firm was busy working on other projects and paid very little attention to this job. To compound matters, they did not stay on top of the requirements of the agreement they had with the prime consultant. As a result of this poor communication, the middle-level consulting firm suddenly became aware that they had to prepare a visual impact analysis for the proposed plant expansion. This was part of their agreement with the prime contractor.

SOL, Inc. was asked by the subcontractor to prepare the visual impact analysis for the plant expansion. SOL, Inc. had never done this kind of work before, but they did not want to disappoint their client (the subcontractor). Therefore, SOL, Inc. agreed to take on the additional work for a slight increase in their contracted amount.

After several weeks of time-consuming, expensive and frustrating work, SOL, Inc. had to tell their subcontractor that they could not produce the visual impact analysis. As a result, the subcontractor had to reassign the project to another consulting firm. SOL, Inc. lost money on the project.

Deliverables

SOL, Inc. successfully completed the land use inventory and socioeconomic analysis for the overall EIS. Their work on these two projects was found to be accurate and complete by the permitting agencies. However, SOL, Inc. lost a substantial amount of money on the project due to their unsuccessful efforts on the visual impact analysis.

The subcontractor with which SOL, Inc. contracted successfully completed their deliverables to the prime contractor, and the plant expansion was eventually approved and built. The subcontractor and the prime contractor made a profit on their work.

Lessons Learned

- *Provide a clearly written comprehensive project scope.* This cannot be overstated. In this particular case, the lack of a clear scope between the prime contractor and the utility was not the problem. The problems began with the lack of agreement on a proper project scope between the subcontractor and SOL, Inc.

- *Good communication must take place throughout the life of a project.* The prime contractor and subcontractor did not communicate well regarding the requirements and schedule for a visual impact analysis. This lack of communication resulted in an emergency for the subcontractor.

- *Do not accept poorly defined and underfunded projects.* SOL, Inc. made the mistake of agreeing to prepare the visual impact analysis even though they had never done one before and there was no scope outlining the required tasks and deliverables. In addition, SOL, Inc. took on the new work with very little additional money to cover the costs. They were too interested in helping the subcontractor get out of a bind and, in the process, ended up losing a substantial amount of money.

- *Always satisfy the client.* Even though many aspects of the overall project were not handled perfectly, the end result was an approved power plant expansion for the utility. The prime contractor, the subcontractor and SOL, Inc. did what needed to be done to bring a quality project in on time. The process was not always pretty and SOL, Inc. lost some money; however, the end result was positive. It should also be noted that SOL, Inc. and the subcontractor went on to successfully and profitably work together on future projects.

CASE STUDY #4: WATER, WATER EVERYWHERE

Background

Central Florida receives an average of 50-60 inches of rainfall per year. Because Florida receives such large amounts of rain, one wouldn't think that water supply would be an issue. In fact, droughts do occur and their impacts can be severe for several reasons:

- Central and south Florida are flat and the rainfall runs off very quickly, ultimately reaching the ocean.

- Due to the flat terrain and intense agricultural and urban land use, there is very little place to store water.

- The population of central and south Florida has grown at a tre-mendous rate and is forecast to continue this rapid rate of growth well into the future. Additional people require additional water.
- Agriculture is a large segment of the local economy and has significant water demands.
- Seasonal influx of "snowbirds" is significant and occurs during the winter dry season when rainfall is at its lowest. This also corresponds with agriculture's highest demand for water.
- The natural environmental resources also require a source of regular and clean water.

Such competing demands, when combined with a drought, can cause serious problems. Sinkholes can occur, crops can be lost, and environmental resources can be irreversibly harmed. In addition, urban users can be asked to cut back on the use of potable water and lawn watering when rains don't come.

The State of Florida is divided into five regional water management districts as established by state statute. Each district has the responsibility of managing the surface and groundwater within its region. In 1997, the Florida legislature passed laws requiring water management districts to prepare long-range, regional water supply plans.

The District decided to prepare regional water supply plans for four geographic regions encompassing the District (see Figure 8-5). The District initiated one of the four regional water supply plans for the Upper East Coast in 1994, prior to adoption of the state requirements for such plans.

The Upper East Coast Water Supply Plan (UECWSP) covers an area of approximately 1,200 square miles and over 300,000 permanent residents. It includes three counties and seven cities. The population for the region is expected to nearly double in the next 20 years. The region is known worldwide for its Indian River citrus products.

The UECWSP was entirely managed and prepared by District staff. Preparation of the plan included the development and application of sophisticated groundwater and surface water computer models. Public input was extensive with over 20 open, advertised public meetings conducted in the region. A UECWSP advisory committee was established consisting of representatives from the local agricultural, environmental and development communities. Elected officials also had seats on the committee. A member of the District's governing board chaired the committee.

Figure 8-5. Water Supply Planning Regions in South Florida

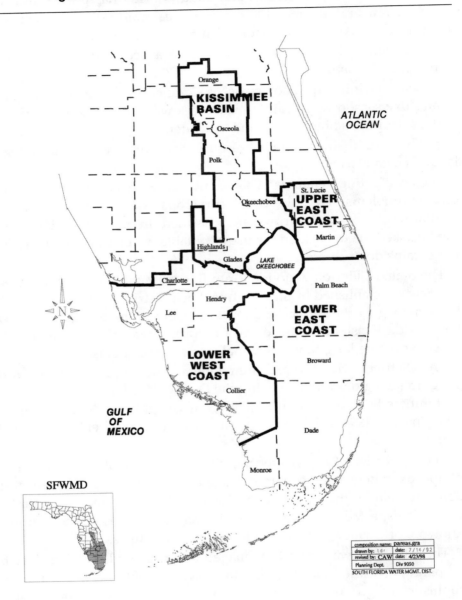

During the middle of the plan's preparation and public input process, the State of Florida passed the requirements for regional water supply plans. As it turned out, the state legislature incorporated the outline and process being used for the UECWSP into the new state law requiring regional water supply plans. Very few changes to the UECWSP were required as a result of the legislative action.

The project team for the UECWSP consisted of multidisciplinary staff from the District. The District used a computerized time-keeping method that provided some minimal tracking assistance to the project manager. The plan took approximately three and one-half years to complete.

Deliverables

The final UECWSP was adopted by the District's governing board in 1998. The plan consists of three documents: the planning document, the background document and appendices. It was the first long-range, regional water supply plan in the state found to be in compliance with the state-mandated water supply planning legislation. An annual UECWSP advisory committee meeting is held to review the status of the plan's implementation.

Lessons Learned

• *Build support and momentum through public participation.* Public participation from the beginning of the planning process through completion provided the support and momentum for final completion and adoption of the plan.

• *Conduct annual implementation meetings.* Conducting annual meetings of the UECWSP advisory committee to report on the implementation of the plan has proven to be very helpful in getting annual budget allocations for implementation projects and is actively supported by the local community.

• *Use a project-focused time-keeping and financial system.* Using the existing internal time accounting and reporting system proved somewhat helpful to the project manager. A modern, project-focused time-keeping and financial system would have provided even more assistance for monitoring and scheduling staff time.

• *Develop an efficient and effective means of getting public input and support.* Over 20 public meetings proved to be overly demanding of staff. At times, it seemed like the project team was spending most of their time preparing for, and responding to, the needs of the advisory committee. In addition, some members of the committee felt that there were too many meetings. A more efficient and effective means of getting public input and support on future plans would be beneficial.

• *Hold a formal, post-project, "lessons learned" meeting.* The project manager and team held a formal "lessons learned" meeting after completion of the plan. This proved to be one of the most helpful and informative aspects of the project. Information gathered from the "lessons learned" session was written and presented to other water supply planning staff and teams.

RESOURCES

South Florida Water Management District. *The Upper East Coast Water Supply Plan, 1999.* West Palm Beach, FL, 1999.

South Florida Water Management District. Web site:
http://www.sfwmd.gov

The Plan to Restore American's Everglades. Web site:
http://www.evergladesplan.org

U.S. Army Corps of Engineers and the South Florida Water Management District. *Central and South Florida (C&SF) Restudy Update,* Number 2. October 1998.

U. S. Army Corps of Engineers, Programs and Project Management Automated Information System. Web site:
http://www.usace.army.mil/inet/functions/cw/cecwb/promis/promisx.htm

9

Perspectives

If you can walk, you can dance.
If you can talk, you can sing.

—ZIMBABWEAN PROVERB

You miss 100% of the shots you never take.

—WAYNE GRETSKY

May the wind always be at your back, and if it isn't, turn around.

—WOODY ALLEN

INTRODUCTION

This chapter offers some advice, guidance and observations about what it means to be a successful planning project manager. In the strictest terms, a project manager's success is determined by his/her ability to bring a quality project in on time and within budget. However, there is more to a project manager's success than that.

If a project manager produces an excellent deliverable, does not exceed time or budget constraints, and the project team despises him and never wants to work with him again, has he been successful? If those three traditional measures are met and the project manager has a nervous breakdown, or his mate and children leave, is he a success?

Being a successful project manager means more than skillfully balancing the three-legged stool of time, resources and scope. Of course, those three basic criteria must be met, but how a project manager meets those project objectives can be just as important in measuring success as the ultimate deliverable outcome.

Chapter 9 presents some thoughts on what constitutes a project manager's success beyond the traditional measures. These ideas and concepts are especially applicable to planners. We have chosen a profession that is geared towards more than bricks and mortar. We are committed to broad goals, aspirations and ideals than cannot be met strictly by physical structures and bureaucratic processes. We are idealists in the truest and best meaning of the word. Planners set high—sometimes impossible—standards, but to do otherwise would be an injustice to our profession and communities.

It is the same with managing projects. As planners managing projects, we must always keep our eyes focused on the horizon and not allow ourselves to get completely wrapped up in just the measurable, quantitative aspects of project management. We need to incorporate the planner's perspective into the way we manage projects.

AFFIRMATIONS

It's All About People

It is so easy to get consumed by project reports, deadlines, constraints and problems that we forget that *projects are people*. Without people, there would be no project. People do all of the work. We rely on machines and other business support systems to get the job done, but it is people who do the work. People collect data, use computers and interact to arrive at solutions.

As project managers, we are ultimately responsible to our team. The team does the hard and tedious work and, as project managers, we can't forget that. Without the team, we would be helpless. Take care of your team and treat them well. The only way a project manager will be successful is if their project team is successful. Do everything you can to make sure they are content and productive.

People are Messy

People are complex organisms. We have physical, mental, emotional and spiritual aspects to our lives. Most of the time, all of our components work reasonably well, but sometimes things get a little out of whack.

We get a speeding ticket on the way into work; we have a fight with our spouse over morning coffee; our kids chuckle, raise their eyebrows and walk out the door when we ask them to do chores. Even more unsettling things can happen, like breaking a leg, losing a loved one or getting divorced.

As human beings, our opportunities for distraction, growth and irritation are limitless. We bring all of these things, to one degree or another, to the workplace. In other words, people are messy. We are not robots that periodically need oiling and new batteries. We are multifaceted, intricately woven masses of contradiction walking around on two legs.

As project managers, we need to recognize that not everyone is up to their very best every day. Most of us, most of the time, do a very good job with what we've been given. Once in a while, the instructions get lost and we need a little leeway. Offering a team member—or the entire team—some slack on one of those days can immeasurably help the individual, the team and the project in the long run. An investment of a little patience and understanding at those times can pay a huge dividend.

Time Takes Time

A project manager cannot acquire 10 years of experience in half the time. It takes at least 10 years to get 10 years of experience. Give yourself some slack if you mess up. It isn't the first time and it won't be the last. Even the most experienced and scar-riddled project manager can make a mistake once in a while. If (or maybe we should say, *when*) you make a mistake, dust yourself off and get back into the game. That is how experience is earned and it takes time.

Maintain Balance

Managing projects can be exhausting, draining and downright hard work. It takes a lot out of a person to be a good project manager. It can be all-encompassing. Successfully bringing in a project can easily overshadow and take precedence over other, healthier activities. At times, it can almost become an obsession.

Remember that it is only a project and the project is only one part of your life. If you lose perspective and let the project manage you, you will become miserable at best, or self-destructive at worst.

It is okay to have fun once in a while. You and the team can benefit by lightening up on occasion. Wear a silly hat to a meeting, have pizza delivered and get goofy t-shirts printed for the project team. You will be amazed at how having fun, even if it is out of character, can invigorate you and the team. It can even make impossible situations tolerable.

If all else fails and you sense that the project is consuming you, try helping another person. Helping someone on the project team or at home can have tremendous benefits to the helper, not just the person receiving the assistance. Providing support to someone in need has the miraculous effect of getting you out of yourself and providing a different outlook on what may have been bothering you.

Take Care of Yourself

The project will not be successful if you run yourself into the ground in the process of trying to manage it. You cannot work on the project 24/7. You need to take care of yourself over the long haul if you and the project are to be a success. "Project manager" is not synonymous with "martyr."

Remember the turtle and the hare? Pace yourself. Planning projects are usually long-term affairs. Sprinting all the time will only burn you out. Proper rest and relaxation on the part of the project manager and team can mean the difference between a successful project and a failure. You cannot manage a project with a nervous breakdown.

CONCLUSION

The purpose of this book was to provide planners with both the technical and practical components of project management. As planners, we are unique. We have a slightly different bent on the world. We are trying to accomplish meaningful improvements that help people.

The traits of a planner are also tremendous assets for a project manager. Being a successful planner is closely related to being a successful project manager. The two share many common characteristics. This book was designed to meld the strengths of a planner with the processes and tools of project management, so that a successful planner could also be a successful project manager.

RESOURCES

Adams, Scott. *The Dilbert Principle: A Cubicle's-Eye View of Bosses, Meetings, Management Fads & Other Workplace Afflictions*. New York, NY: HarperCollins, 1996.

Brown, Karen A. "Developing Project Management Skills: A Service Learning Approach." *Project Management Journal*, December 2000, pp. 53-58.

Catlette, Bill and Richard Hadden. *Contented Cows Give Better Milk*. Germantown, TN: Saltillo Press, 2000.

Covey, Stephen R. *Principle-Centered Leadership*. New York, NY: Simon & Schuster, 1991.

Flannes, Steven W. and Ginger Levin. *People Skills for Project Managers*. Management Concepts, 2001.

Index